Buddhist
Wisdom

for daily living

Buddhist Wisdom

for daily living

Christopher Titmuss

WALKING STICK PRESS
Cincinnati, Ohio

First published in Great Britain in 2001
by Godsfield Press Ltd
Godsfield House, Old Alresford
Hampshire SO24 9RQ, UK

First published in North America
in 2001 by Walking Stick Press
an imprint of F&W Publications, Inc.
1507 Dana Avenue
Cincinnati, OH 45207
1–800/289–0963

ISBN 1-58297-090-4

2 4 6 8 10 9 7 5 3 1

© 2001 Godsfield Press
Text © 2001 Christopher Titmuss

Picture Research by Lynda Marshall
Illustrations by Andrew Kulman, Andrew Lawes, and Sally Smith

Index compiled by Indexing Specialists

Designed for Godsfield Press by
The Bridgewater Book Company

Christopher Titmuss asserts the moral right to be
identified as the author of this work.

Printed and bound in Hong Kong

The publishers wish to thank the following for the use of photographs:
Corbis: pp. 2, 5, 7, 9, 11, 14, 21, 22, 23, 27, 29, 33, 35, 36, 37, 41, 42, 44, 45, 47, 49, 51, 55, 57,
59, 61, 64, 65, 66, 68, 71, 73, 74, 76, 77, 78, 82, 84, 87, 88, 89, 91, 92, 93, 95, 96, 97, 98, 101, 105, 108,
109, 110, 111, 112, 115, 120, 121, 127, 129, 130, 131, 132, 135, 139, 140, 141, 143, 145, 147, 150,
151, 152, 154; **GettyOneStone**: pp. 53, 126; **Lynda Myers**: pp. 28, 58, 72, 102, 107, 116,
133, 144, 156; **NASA**: p. 67; **Stock Market**: pp. 20, 46, 69, 106, 117, 119, 123,
124, 125, 134; **Telegraph Colour Library**: p. 153.

Contents

INTRODUCTION: a guide to *Buddhist Wisdom for Daily Living*

Between 1970–76, I spent six years as a Buddhist monk in Thailand and India. I regard this period as my time as a student in the University of Life. Some people believe that life in a rural Buddhist monastery is an escape from reality. In my experience, it seemed far from it. I found myself living with between 100 and 200 monks and nuns, none of whom I knew. We were together seven days a week, morning, noon, and night, through the cool season, the hot season, and the monsoon. Sometimes we got on well with each other and sometimes we did not. Not even the teacher, Venerable Ajahn Dhammadaro, the Abbot of Wat Chai Na (Monastery at the End of the Rice Paddy) stood above criticism. It was a challenging and precious period in my life.

By conventional standards, we led an austere life, permitted only a handful of possessions, including two sets of robes, a begging bowl, a razor, and a water filter. We ate only in the morning and fasted daily from 12 noon for the next 19 hours. Apart from meetings with the teachers, we spent many hours in silence and meditated in the formal sitting, walking, and standing postures. The teachings and the practices gave us the opportunity to go deep into ourselves and to look deeply into existence. We had stripped our life down to the barest essentials for this opportunity. Not surprisingly, some of the senior monks regarded pursuit of career, money, and position, and hours of television watching throughout most evenings, as an escape from reality.

For many, a Buddhist monastery in a remote area of Southeast Asia would seem a world far removed from today's intense and busy society. Yet, I found a wealth of teachings and practices eminently suitable for daily life, for working men and women who need the tools to live wisely. Since I left the monastery and disrobed, I have had the privilege of sharing the teachings of the Buddha annually around the world through hosting retreats and writing books.

*The Buddha image serves as a reminder
of the important function that meditation
plays in spiritual life.*

*I believe the voice of the Buddha matters as much today as it did 2,500 years ago, when
he offered his teachings in northern India to a relatively sophisticated and cultured people,
to help them realize wisdom for daily life. I regard myself as a small bridge between the
monastery and the householder's life. Like many readers, I have all the usual
responsibilities: I have bills to pay, including a mortgage on my modest home in Totnes
in Devon in England; I am in a relationship; I am a parent; I am a trustee of a charity;
a co-founder and fund-raiser for a school in India; I spend most days of the year dealing
with people's personal problems, as well as answering countless letters and emails. So, I can
share with readers many of their concerns and issues.*

As you read through Buddhist Wisdom for Daily Living, *you will see that I have
drawn upon the words of the Buddha and highlighted areas that men and women have to
face in daily life.*

How to use this book

I would suggest that you read the book through at your own pace from cover to cover to familiarize yourself with some of the themes. I have written this book with three kinds of people in mind:

❖ People who simply wish to develop practical resources to deal well with daily life circumstances
❖ People who wish to find out the relevance of Buddhist wisdom in today's society
❖ People who are already established on a spiritual path and wish to go more deeply into the breadth and depth of the path

I have written a brief introduction to each chapter to provide you with an overview of its contents. Each chapter also includes two meditations and two practices to be applied. Some of the practices take the form of a reflection, while other practices suggest something particular to do during the day.

There are two ways you can approach this book. One is to make it a practice manual. You might devote one week to each chapter, initially reading through it slowly and carefully, seeking the points that relate primarily to your experiences during that week. Endeavor to apply one or two features of the teachings during the course of the week to see what works for you. In the formal meditation posture, whether in an upright chair, stool, or meditation cushion, read slowly and mindfully through the guided meditation. If the guided meditation feels particularly relevant, then read it through slowly several times until some of the simple and beneficial truths of the meditation run deep into your heart. I have offered two practices for each day. They are not easy, and you may wish to keep a journal of your responses. Your journal can serve as a record of what you are learning from the teachings and ways to see situations from different perspectives. There is a certain discipline involved in all of this, but if you can regard the practices as a challenge rather than a tiresome task, you will eventually experience the beneficial fruits of your commitment.

It is not necessary to go systematically through each chapter giving a week to each. You may find that one chapter stands out in terms of its relevance to your daily life. You may wish to concentrate on that chapter for weeks or even months, if necessary, until you feel you have absorbed its benefits. Some of the other meditations and daily practices elsewhere in the book may work for you better with a particular chapter so do be willing to mix and match!

I remember years ago, the Dalai Lama kindly came to speak to participants in a retreat that I gave in Bodh Gaya, India, where the Buddha was enlightened. He told those at the retreat that if Buddhist practices did not work, then to explore other spiritual traditions and religions. To readers, I would suggest that you explore these practices first for only a year. If you experience no real benefits, then keep exploring the spiritual path in other ways. In a celebrated talk, the Buddha said that we can know the fulfillment of the Path to Enlightenment in seven days of dedicated practice. Enlightenment may be closer than you think!

Christopher Titmuss

Mindful reading of sacred texts can provide insight into the quality and direction of our lives.

Mindfulness of Problems and Solutions

Divine Vehicle is a name for the Noble Eightfold Path.
It is the vehicle of the Dharma.
The Path culminates in the expulsion of greed, hate, and delusion.

THE BUDDHA

In this chapter, we give priority to attending to the pressures that we put on ourselves in daily life. We learn to recognize the arising of the judgmental mind that makes our life difficult, so that we do not keep undermining ourselves. We learn to see it as a brief reaction, not giving it power to affect our natural well-being.

This chapter includes the eight factors of the Noble Eightfold Path, taught by the Buddha. It is worthwhile to remember each factor so that you develop every link of the path in your daily life. You will see important aspects of the Eightfold Path covered throughout the book. Remember the practice points to awakening, and realizing the mind of a Buddha, not becoming a Buddhist, mean you discover an enlightened life rather than adopt new religious beliefs.

We also practice working on our heart. A person with a healthy inner life knows and experiences much connection with and gratitude for daily life. Unfortunately, our heart easily neglects the capacity that every person has to develop such appreciative joy.

The chapter concludes with two meditations, *Meditation on Happiness* and *Meditation on Dharma* (Dharma means teachings and practices that contribute to our deepest welfare and our Buddha mind). Sit in an upright posture, then quietly and slowly read the two meditations so that your inner life has the opportunity to respond respectfully to the here and now.

The Buddha pointed out a plain truth of existence: suffering exists. It is real, not unreal, but wisdom dissolves suffering. He spent 45 years in northern India, from the age of 35 to 80, pointing out the direct way to the resolution of suffering. He said that we are not helpless when we encounter the problems of daily life. He described himself as a physician providing a remedy for the variety of difficulties that we have to face in the course of our existence.

There are often many pressures in our daily life. We sometimes feel that circumstances drive us along, and it seems hard to direct our life in the way that we would wish. Our various roles, responsibilities, and financial commitments keep us on a treadmill from one day to the next. When we look at our circumstances, we see that we exert pressure upon ourselves as well as trying to fulfill the expectations that others have of us. If others are not giving us a hard time, we find that we give ourselves one.

We might keep telling ourselves that things should not be like this. Such thoughts make little difference when we drive ourselves along from one set of tasks to another. So we keep experiencing the cost of an unexamined life, of living in an unmindful way. There is a significant loss of peace of mind, loss of inner contentment, and loss of happiness with the way that our life is going.

There are other consequences as well. We never seem to meet up to our own expectations. The more we strive, the more discontent we feel. Not knowing any other way, we imagine that once we have completed a particular task, we will create a real breathing space in our life. No wonder we have become slaves to desire. Living wisely enables us to approach important features of our daily life in a different and enlightened way.

FAULT-FINDING

The Buddha's teachings emphasize the examination of the self, of the ego, and its impact on daily life. The self often pushes itself to succeed because it cannot find success in the present. It is vital that we acknowledge these feelings of lack of self-worth, which express themselves in a variety of ways. These include the following thoughts:

❖ I am not good enough
❖ I am stupid
❖ I am not good at anything
❖ I cannot be loved
❖ They are better/more beautiful than I
❖ I am not worth being noticed

You may recognize something of yourself in any of these phrases. They work like a virus in our inner life, consuming natural happiness and contentment. It is often much easier for us to detail what we do not like about ourselves rather than what we appreciate. If we were to write a list of what we do not like about ourselves physically, emotionally, and mentally, we could probably fill a couple of pages quite easily. If we were to write a list of what we appreciate about ourselves physically, emotionally, and mentally, we might find ourselves rather hard pressed to fill half a page, let alone two pages. This difficulty in finding

At times, we get caught up in finding fault with ourselves. We experience a lack of self-worth.

13

positive things reflects the ingrained negative attitude that we have toward ourselves.

When we cannot cope with the faults we find with ourselves, we easily project these faults onto others. It then becomes a habit to see only what we do not like about other people, not only strangers but also people who matter to us. What we do not like about others may reflect what we do not like about ourselves. When this habit becomes particularly entrenched, we end up cynical about everyone. We will find no happiness if we look at the world through such colored glasses.

Our tendency to react to difficult situations stops us from seeing things clearly. The Buddha's teachings point the way to seeing things clearly so that we transform unsatisfactory states of mind into clarity, calmness, and understanding of situations. This quickness to react shows a lack of clarity.

On other occasions, we get so angry with ourselves that we end up feeling despair at what we have done or neglected to do. We believe all the negative thoughts toward ourselves, as though there is something valid and genuine about them. That small, inner voice of concern may arise that questions this painful interpretation of others, ourselves, and situations affecting our lives. The first step is learning to listen to that small voice until you find that it becomes much louder.

If we forget to remind ourselves of fresh ways of looking at a situation, we will become prisoners of our own mind. The Buddha made a poignant remark when he once commented that no one can do us as much harm as our own ill-directed mind. One of the most important choices that we can make involves changing any perceptions, views, and reactions that keep making life difficult for others and ourselves.

The Buddha pointed out that we often do not realize how blind we are to what we experience, and this causes suffering. He said that once a king invited

PRACTICES FOR TODAY 1

1

Make appreciation a theme for today

2

If you see or hear something that you appreciate, stop and give it your full attention

3

If you complete a task, then stop to feel that sense of appreciation, before going on to something else

4

If you hear a kind word toward yourself, acknowledge it, do not dismiss it

5

Take a few minutes to be aware of the expanse of life between sky and earth

Exposure and mindfulness to open spaces contributes to putting our personal life issues into a proper perspective.

the blind people in the city of Savvatthi in India to place their hands on different parts of an elephant. One thought the tusk was a post; another thought the skin was a basket; another thought the foot was the base of a pillar; another thought the rump was mortar. Then they began to quarrel. None of them could see clearly, the Buddha pointed out, and this inevitably led them to conflict.

THE SOLVING OF THE PROBLEM

There are four practical steps that we can make when we are problem-solving:

❖ The Buddhist tradition advises that we wake up to what is going on within ourselves. This means becoming acutely aware of our tendency toward self-blame and finding fault with others. We practice letting go of destructive views for as long as it takes to be at peace with ourselves.
❖ Remember that one particular feature of ourselves or others can never be a statement about the whole person.
❖ Acknowledge how hard it is to change these negative patterns yet not submit to them.
❖ Practice to find ways to express appreciation for ourselves and others as an antidote to fault-finding.

When you first start expressing something different from negativity, you will experience these expressions as false, even unreal. This is due to the degree of identification you have with the feeling of lack of self-worth, or because you are used to seeing this lack of self-worth in others. Negativity and cynicism come from these unresolved feelings within.

When we are immersed in such negative patterns, we do not want to admit that we feel and think this way. There is a concern that if we share such experiences with others, it will alarm them. They might think that we are cracking up or experiencing some serious emotional problems. Fear of admitting to ourselves or to others our lack of self-acceptance only reinforces this particular difficulty.

We forget that this lack of self-worth is one of the most widespread problems of all and that it needs to be brought to the surface. Transforming the inner life is like putting vegetables in hot water to cook them and watching the scum come to the surface. It is a necessary part of the process of changing our inner life.

Our efforts to try harder and harder to achieve our goals certainly do not provide the answer. A sense of worth comes through living wisely, not through the demands of the self.

So we make a clear resolution to explore the four steps detailed before as part of a journey toward inner contentment and clarity in our relationships with others. The Buddhist tradition uses widely the concept of *practice*. Practice means application of such steps every week, even every day. At times, it may seem like we are going two steps forward and one step backward as we learn the value of self-acceptance, acceptance of others, and developing a different attitude to situations.

EXPANDING THE HEART

We commit daily to applying the four steps to overcome self-rejection and negativity toward others. We also practice working on our heart. It is all too easy to take the view: "There is nothing to appreciate in my life. Others have all the luck. They just seem to be happy but I'm not like that." Again, we are stuck with the old mind-set that believes that our inner life has become fixed and has no capacity for inner change. The four steps need to be applied to this view as well.

One of the healthy antidotes to the problem of self-rejection is appreciative joy, an invaluable emotional response that we can practice. A person with a healthy inner life knows and experiences much appreciation in daily life. Unfortunately, our heart can easily neglect our ability to develop appreciative joy. The Buddha refers to such joy as a state of divine abiding. In other words, he gives it the same significance as a religious person would to living with God, or experiencing the true divinity of life.

Why is appreciative joy so significant for human existence? If we examine some of our typical attitudes, we often notice that there is a degree of

To a degree, a rose mirrors the realities of life—the great beauty of the flower and the thorns we need to treat with care and respect.

dissatisfaction. A young lawyer told me that when she started work for a law firm, she joined on the same day as another young woman from the same university with the same degree. After a year, she received an increase in salary that pleased her very much. Then she found out that her colleague had received an even bigger pay rise. She lost all appreciation for her own wage increase and the achievement it represented and felt very envious of her colleague. Her envy sparked feelings of self-rejection and she began to feel that she was not good enough.

She then began to reflect on what was good about working for the company. She wrote a list of her appreciations, read them several times to herself, and acknowledged that her colleague deserved a bigger increase given the number of hours she put in at the office. At first, she felt exploited but then realized she had every reason to accept the differences in salary.

We need to practice appreciative joy at the achievements of others so that we overcome envy and resentment. Such a practice enables us to keep in touch with each other rather than becoming dependent on approval from others. Such experiences of pleasure become increasingly short-lived as we find ourselves constantly trying to secure more and more attention for ourselves.

Appreciative joy, a feature of the heart that the Buddha refers to often, acts as an antidote to the pursuit of short-term pleasure. It reminds us to stop and delight in life. It is worth noticing that often what we appreciate we cannot own or have a claim over: for example, when we take an evening walk and look up at the night sky and experience the wonder and mystery of the Milky Way; when we see a beautiful bird on the wing, swooping and gliding across the sky on a summer's afternoon; or when we wake up in the morning and witness the first frost of the winter and that sharp coldness that grips the morning air.

We cannot buy these experiences nor organize them, but a deepening appreciation for the wonders of daily life reduces this obsession with pursuing more and more pleasure.

MAKING A DAILY RESOLUTION

A man came to see me for a one-to-one meeting. He was experiencing intense jealousy. His wife had abruptly left him for another man with whom she said she had fallen hopelessly in love. She had moved out of their apartment and in with her new lover. The man who visited me told me that it tortured him every night to think that she could be so happy in the arms of another.

I spoke to him about the importance of making a daily resolution to let go of the past, to let go of clinging, and making the daily determination to get on with his own life. He also needed to cultivate appreciation for the space available to him to make a fresh start in his own life.

A few days later he contacted me again and told me that he had tried the meditations on appreciative joy I had advised him to do, but did not get anything out of them, and so had stopped. I reminded him that

Plants and weeds grow together. Wisdom is discerning what to cultivate and what to discard.

I had said several times to him that he must practice, and that practice takes time. It can often take months, perhaps years, to learn a new skill. I suggested to him that he go back again to developing appreciative joy through four or five meditations every week for at least a year and a day. If he had not gained any deep benefit after that time, then he would be in the position to say they were not working for him.

All too often, we want an instant answer and resolution to a problem; however this is not always possible. Yes, of course, we can experience an utterly transforming moment, free from development in time, but often, for most of us, we need to get on with practical inner development in order to live wisely. If we practice, then appreciation and gladness will not become an occasional event but a daily experience associated with simply being alive and joy for the happiness of others.

There is much that is cruel and obscene in this world, but equally there is much to gladden the heart and touch deep places of joy—let us make all of this wonderfully clear to ourselves.

FORMING RIGHT RELATIONSHIPS

The Buddha's teachings refer to the Noble Eightfold Path. He calls the path "noble" because a person who follows diligently and respectfully all the links in the Eightfold Path lives a noble life. He reminds us frequently that we cannot become noble through wealth, title, or privilege. The Noble Eightfold Path consists of right understanding, right intention, right speech, right action, right livelihood, right effort, right mindfulness, and right meditative concentration. If the Buddha were alive today, he would probably call it the Noble Ninefold Path, and add right relationship, although it is found indirectly in right understanding, right intention, and right speech.

During a group meeting in Sarnath, India, where the Buddha gave his first teachings, I remember discussing the nature of a freedom and joy that takes full responsibility for our roles and commitments with a group of forty people from around the world. One person from the US expressed the commonly held view that being in a committed relationship makes it extraordinarily difficult to know and experience complete freedom. The American said that as long as we have a partner or children, or both, or care for elderly parents, we can never be free. He added that this was the reason why the Buddha encouraged people to become monks or nuns to get away from such roles and responsibilities.

I responded that caring relationships lacked the power to tie us down but expressed an opportunity to love another. Our attitude of mind can imprison us, not daily contact with loved ones. I told him that we need to examine what constitutes right relationship and what generates problems around our perceptions of our relationships with others.

In examining the issue of right relationship, we agreed that three considerations mattered:

❖ Addressing unresolved issues and the way these have a harmful influence over a relationship. Trying to get our own way places great pressure on another and as result, the other person will either submit out of fear, get angry, or withdraw.

❖ Looking at our need for approval. This often causes much unrest in a relationship, when we have a constant expectation that another ought to give us all the attention and acknowledgment that we feel we deserve.

❖ Examining our need to feel understood. We have to learn to listen to each other and need to develop communication skills. Our intention, tone of voice, and language matter equally.

Sometimes, it seems we can never do nor say the right thing. Motivations and intentions get questioned. We then feel that the misunderstanding is growing, and that makes us resentful. Our need to be understood

When meditating, find a comfortable position in which to sit. Keep your back straight and breathe deeply.

*Warm, clear, and considerate
intentions take priority when we
communicate with another person.*

then acts as a block to a clear communication. When we feel misunderstood, we may find ourselves bursting into tears as a result. Two people then become like two ships passing in the night, not able to see each other clearly. Neither can comprehend the other. We have to practice to meet each other half-way.

The Buddha's emphasis on mindfulness of our interconnection with each other reduces significantly the inflammatory remarks that can spring from mutual misunderstanding. It cannot be overstated how important this area is if we are to follow a noble, mindful path. Once again, we learn to express appreciation for another when we feel understood. The capacity to acknowledge places of harmony and agreement provides us with the stability and

confidence we need to look into those areas of discord or disharmony.

If you are willing to listen to the other person and attend to them as fully as possible then you can resolve all types of problems and difficulties. Happiness in our lives springs from knowing that we live in right relationship with others.

The Buddha says that everybody has one thing in common: the wish to be happy. It doesn't matter who we are, what society we live in, or what our background and upbringing is: we all share the wish to be happy. It seems that some people genuinely live a very happy life, while others seem to experience a great deal of unhappiness, and others experience both happiness and unhappiness at a fairly even level.

You might conclude that some are born lucky and others are not—as if birth and childhood determined everything. If that had real truth to it, there would be no point in making any choices about anything since our upbringing would determine the outcome.

KEYS TO HAPPINESS

What makes people happy on a sustainable basis? We may be fortunate enough to know somebody who genuinely appears happy from one day to the next, despite the difficulties and hardships they may experience. Such a person can share their attitude toward life, but if you asked them, "Why are you always so happy?" they may find it difficult to give a clear and comprehensive answer. To find happiness, we can try cultivating the following typical responses until we experience the same natural wisdom:

❖ I just take everything as it comes

❖ I live one day at a time

❖ I have learned not to have too many expectations of others or myself

❖ As long as I can spend some time out of doors, I feel connected with life and do not want too much from it

❖ I regard everything that happens to me as a gift or a challenge

❖ I try to appreciate much and want little

How often do we witness the birth of a new day? It is a truly wonderful process taking place.

All of these responses show a genuine wisdom about living on this earth. They may seem rather bland answers if we are looking for some deep philosophical interpretation on how to be happy. What we forget is that those immediate responses of happy people carry a deep truth to them. They are living their life according to that basic understanding and they feel the benefit in their feelings and thoughts.

Others who do not accept things as they come, or do not know to live one day at a time, find themselves living in a painful dream world of their own mental creations about past and future, likes and dislikes. There is very little chance for deep happiness and contentment if we live in a dream world. The truth will shatter our dreams and fantasies.

Happiness is not a gift from the gods, nor born from good fortune, nor from a satisfactory upbringing, but an emerging understanding about living in tune with the way things are, rather than the projections of how you demand things to be. If you reflect a little over any recent experiences of happiness, you will probably notice within yourself a sense of harmony, not only with your own life but with your world, with what surrounds you.

This experience of happiness enables us to know a harmonious inner life and, once again, that all-important appreciation for the ordinary things that easily go unnoticed when the self is obsessing over various circumstances.

At the end of meditations in the Buddhist tradition, it is commonly said, "May all beings be happy." Sometimes nonBuddhists wonder why this is said when Buddhists do not believe in a god who controls the universe and permits pleasure and pain on sentient life. However, this refrain expresses a deep intention of happiness since it is the core wish of everybody.

PRACTICES FOR TODAY 2

1

Make a commitment to memorize all factors of the Noble Eightfold Path

2

Reflect on the Noble Eightfold Path as a resource for living wisely

3

Focus today on one factor and apply it to a situation

4

Reflect afterward on the significance of its application

5

Examine right understanding, the first link: "What do I need to understand today?"

An expansive and far-reaching appreciation for the diversity of life contributes to our well-being.

Daily happiness is possible for those who develop wisely an outlook toward life that contributes to inner peace and joy, and who practice to overcome what blocks it. Sometimes we may think, "What have I got to be unhappy about? What have I got to complain about?" Such thoughts usually indicate that we are clinging on to an issue and refuse to move on from it.

Finally, without even getting up from the spot where you are reading this page, take a moment out to have a quiet meditative look all around you and acknowledge how much you have to be happy about in your life. Let that feeling sink in well and deeply, so that you feel nourished through your appreciation of what is already present.

Tibetan monks chant the words of the Buddha beneath a large shady tree in Bodh Gaya, India.

ATTENDING A RETREAT

In order to create meditative silence, it may be necessary to go on a retreat, to sort out our priorities, to focus on them, to discover vision. The Buddha said that after his enlightenment under the bodhi tree in Bodh Gaya, he had a vision. He realized that there is suffering in this world and, most importantly, he realized through his own experience the resolution of this suffering. Despite some temporary doubt, he kept faith with his vision, and for the next 45 years he walked the length and breadth of northern India sharing his vision with others, namely the complete and utter resolution of suffering through wisdom and liberation. Everything that he said and all the various choices that he made related in some way or other to this vision. For more than 2,500 years, he has inspired others to take up this vision.

Meditation on Happiness

Sit with a straight back in a quiet place. Slowly and mindfully read the meditation and then spend several minutes silently absorbing the reading. Then read it slowly through again at the end of the meditation. Repeat as often as it feels appropriate.

Allow twenty minutes for this meditation and then gradually expand the period of time over days or weeks. You can always tape this meditation or any of the others and listen to it in formal meditation times. You can adapt the language of these meditations to suit what feels appropriate to you. Always make sure that you use precise language, not emotive language that can work against insight and understanding.

I am relaxing on the inbreath, I am relaxing on the outbreath

I am mindful of my outbreath when my mind easily wanders

I am relaxing on the outbreath

I am staying upright while allowing the mind to rest in the body

I am allowing the brain cells to become quiet, to feel the harmony of the mind with the body

I feel happy that I am mindfully breathing in

I feel happy that I am mindfully breathing out

I feel happy to have this opportunity to be still

I feel happy to have this opportunity to be silent

I feel happy to have this opportunity to be here and now

I feel happy to be alive

Right now, there is nothing that I want

Right now, there is nothing that I have to pursue

Right now, I am happy to breathe in

Right now, I am happy to breathe out

Right now, there is nothing to add to this moment

Right now, there is nothing to subtract from this moment

Right now, I am happy breathing in

Right now, I am happy breathing out

Sitting and meditating on the simple pleasure of just being alive can bring great and lasting peace.

*The beautiful sight of a rainbow can lighten the life
as the Dharma can, illuminating the body and mind.*

Meditation on the Dharma

The Dharma refers to teachings and practices that
point directly to an enlightened life. The teachings
give support to all through providing us with the
resources to transform our lives. To see the Dharma is
to see the Buddha. This meditation reminds us of the
importance of the Dharma for our daily lives and of
contact with those (called the Sangha) who practice
the Dharma in order to live a noble way of life. Read
this meditation on the Dharma, reflect on your
commitment to the Dharma, and spend several
minutes in silence, mindful of the Dharma of the
here and now.

Nobody will enlighten my life
I cannot enlighten my life
A Buddha cannot enlighten my life
A Buddha can only point out the way
  through the jungle of confused ideas
  and troublesome mind states

Only the Dharma can enlighten my life
Therefore I prostrate before the Dharma
Make myself a servant of the Dharma
I can only pay respect to the Dharma
  through the pure and clear activities of
  my body, speech and mind
I practice to dissolve the differences
  through notions of superior and inferior Dharmas
So that the Dharma and the Buddha abide
  inseparably like honey and sweetness
I practice the Dharma through morality
That means nonharming and nonexploitation
  of others and of myself, too
I practice the Dharma through being mindful
  and meditating on things that matter
I practice the Dharma through living wisely
  uprooting the force of selfish desire
  embracing all that enters into my life with clarity
  and allowing the Dharma to be my guide and refuge
For to follow these important principles is to
  abide among the Buddhas

Mindfulness of Diet and Body

Mindfulness of body is established,
to the extent of bare knowing and recollection,
while abiding independent, and not clinging.

THE BUDDHA

We usually eat three times a day. Pressures in other areas of our life affect our eating habits, and our eating habits affect other areas of our life. It is easy to become obsessive around food.

We develop a practice of establishing for ourselves a nutritious diet of food and drink so that alcohol or food used purely for pleasure does not detract from a balanced diet. We consider what we eat, the amount we need, and engage in the practice of mindfulness of eating.

One of the hardest disciplines is regular exercise. We have many good intentions in this area of physical life, but we need that extra determination for intention to lead to activity. As the benefit develops, we find that the desire to exercise starts to come to us naturally. We are making the journey from effort to effortlessness.

The Buddha said that the greatest wealth is health. A healthy mind contributes significantly to a healthy body. We all know how easy it is to take health for granted. There are many ways that we can contribute to our health but we have to learn to work with periods of sickness that can arise through countless conditions.

At the end of the chapter, there are two meditations, *Meditation on Healing* and *Meditation on Acceptance*.

The Buddha paid little attention to diet. He adopted a flexible attitude toward eating animals, birds, and fish. In modern as in ancient India, householders only feed wandering monks, nuns, and ascetics a vegetarian diet as it is considered the kind of food most appropriate for the spiritual life, and most people in rural India today remain vegetarian.

We should not forget that the kitchen is a central place in the home, and the center of the kitchen is often the refrigerator. It is all too easy to make too many pilgrimages to this shrine in the home, and instead of food giving us nourishment and simple pleasure, we make a problem out of it. Authorities on diet remind us what to eat and what not to eat. We are told that some foodstuffs are good in one way but not in another.

We are all familiar with the view that we are what we eat, but though this rhetoric might be expressed frequently, what does it actually mean? We cannot deny the impact that our diet has on our life. Times have changed dramatically since the time of the Buddha. We overeat, undereat, eat unhealthy food, and experience anxiety and guilt around food. We are unsure about foods containing high cholesterol and animal products, as well as processed food and genetically modified food.

Several years ago, a friend of mine in Massachusetts, USA, went to see her physician who told her that her stomach pains and struggle with her weight had nothing whatsoever to do with her diet. The doctor claimed that her health problems were due to hereditary and genetic factors, and had nothing to do with lifestyle. He claimed also that it was only a matter of time before medical science found the right medication to dissolve fattening foods as they entered the digestive system. He anticipated that within a generation or two we would be able to eat what we liked, secure in the knowledge that medical science would provide tablets to help the body to expel and sort out anything that might be bad for us.

Many of us would disagree with the view that medical science will eventually have the capacity to control our health in such a way. There are millions of people who experience serious health issues directly related to diet so it seems important to take time to reflect on our relationship with food. There are four primary considerations regarding food, and all four matter equally. They are:

❖ What we eat
❖ The amount we eat
❖ The quality of mindfulness when we eat
❖ Emotional influences at the time of eating

If we can bear in mind each of these four considerations, we can discover a balanced relationship to food, rather than overeating, undereating, compulsive eating, or experiencing anxiety around food.

WHAT WE EAT

We need to commit to a daily discipline of eating a nutritious and healthy diet, and ensure that the food we eat and drink for pleasure, such as chocolate, cake, and coffee, does not act as a substitute for our basic diet. Getting this balance clear can make all the difference. Nutritionists keep reminding us of the importance of a balanced diet with fruit, vegetables, grains, and protein at the center, and it is important that we take notice of their advice. No one else can do this for us, or for our families.

If we are parents, we will have to resist the intense pressure from our children to feed them fast food, sweets, sugary drinks, fries, and chips. Part of our responsibility as parents is to protect our children from their own desires. Most children do not have the

Instead of always going to the supermarket, we can go to local shops and markets, similar to this one in India, to find inexpensive and exotic foods.

PRACTICES FOR TODAY 1

1
Make one meal today a meditation

2
Eat mindfully, slowly, chewing the food

3
Handle cutlery with mindfulness

4
Be rather still and silent, without reading material

5
Before leaving the table, express appreciation inwardly for the food

wisdom to know what is good for them and when inactive they will keep nibbling away.

There are lifelong consequences for this in terms of health and sense of self-worth. Inactivity for adults and children is a causal factor for overeating. Using the television as a baby-sitter and offering fizzy drinks, chips, and ice-cream becomes a means to keep them quiet rather than supporting their development through fun, play, and creative initiatives.

Adults and children are much more likely to want to eat a good meal when they have been active, and have used their bodies for running, jumping, and playing games. Having burned off all the energy from the previous meal, we are then ready for another healthy one later on.

There is a fear among some adults that cutting down, or cutting out, meat and fish from the diet would create protein deficiency. However, protein is in a variety of sources, and it only takes a little reading, some advice from a nutritionist, or information from the Internet, to see that vegetarians in general live a healthier and longer life.

In Britain, it is reported that more than one thousand people per day become committed vegetarians. In particular, more and more teenagers have made the choice to stop eating the flesh of animals, birds, and fish, and in future years, today's teenagers will be making the decision on what goes on the meal table of their homes.

For some people, the decision to become vegetarian arises from a moral concern for the rights of animals, while for others, there are health concerns. For example, fish are contaminated as they live in polluted seas; farm animals regularly receive injections to fatten them up, or receive questionable animal feed. In Britain, more than 600 million animals and birds are eaten every year. It is worthwhile reflecting upon a vegetarian diet or reducing the amount of meat and fish we eat.

OUR RELATIONSHIP WITH FOOD

The Buddha pointed out that there are four kinds of nutrient: food, contact, intention, and consciousness. If we nourish ourselves through contact with good friends, constructive intentions, and conscious living, it will contribute significantly to a balanced relationship to food. We also bring conscious attention to our diet. It is all too easy to draw the conclusion that people simply have to eat less, but that is not the only answer. The other three considerations all matter equally. Some people do not have to eat less. They can continue to eat the same amount of food but should remember to eat the right *kinds* of food.

Food can easily become a poor compensation for unhappiness and discontent in our emotional life. One woman wryly commented at a weight watcher's club, during her struggles to keep her weight under control, that "I am digging my grave with a knife and fork."

If we remember to eat the right food, the stomach can still feel reasonably full after meal times. Weight loss will take the pressure off the heart, lungs, and organs. It is common knowledge that there is inner satisfaction in having a balanced relationship with food, and contentment arises when we feel comfortable with our weight and at home with our bodies. Although it is not easy because we are not used to it, we should try to leave a little space in our stomachs after we have eaten to enable the food to digest more easily. We should also try to leave around three hours between eating a main meal in the evening and going to sleep. A full stomach just before bedtime prevents proper rest, as the digestive system keeps on working while we sleep.

In order to diet or eat the right food at the right time, we may need the support of others to provide an extra link of connection until the discipline around food becomes an effortless appreciation for wise living. It is possible to make that transition and we will feel all the better for it if we can do it.

EATING WITH MINDFULNESS

The Buddhist tradition has wisely emphasized the importance of bringing mindfulness to everything that we do, including our diet. Mindfulness is a key feature of the Buddha's teachings. All those who love the spiritual life are encouraged to live mindfully in all areas of life and this includes eating, drinking, chewing, tasting, urinating, and defecating. Living a mindful life covers the whole process from the first bite of food to its elimination.

What is mindfulness of eating? Firstly, we engage in a quiet reflection on the interconnection of food with everything else. Farmers, trucks and trains, packagers, staff in shops, and supermarkets all act as links in the international food chain, as do the land, water, and air that enables food to grow. There is a vast chain of interconnection by the time food arrives on the plate in front of us, and it is worth spending a few moments in reflection and appreciation for all those people who make it possible for us to eat. Try the following meditation:

May all those who have contributed to the food chain live in peace and harmony. May their families and friends be well and happy. May the energy that comes from this meal contribute to the welfare of others, near and far.

To eat mindfully, keep the back reasonably straight and upright so that there is some expansion in the stomach area, enabling the digestive processes to work easily. If we are alone, we can make a meal a genuine moment-to-moment act of mindfulness. To eat a meal in a silent and conscious way becomes a meditation.

We eat only the amount of food that is appropriate, and remember from the beginning to keep faith with the discipline of knowing when enough is enough. At the end of the meal we again express gratitude for the food, and remember to share our many blessings in daily life, including access to food at any time. Deep kindness and generosity then emerge from mindful eating with thoughtful reflection.

If we go to a restaurant we may find that the amount of food we are offered is far beyond our need. It is worthwhile to ask for an extra plate so we can

Buddhist tradition has a great love of natural beauty. A flower in full bloom is a mandala of the wonder of life.

Regular contact with the natural world nourishes our sense of a deep interconnection with everything around us.

put aside what we know we do not need to eat. Most restaurants provide a small disposable container to take extra food home in to eat the following day. These modest gestures of mindful eating contribute to an overall sense of well-being.

FOOD AND OUR EMOTIONS

Our emotional life plays an important part in our relationship to food. It might be too simplistic to say that if we are unhappy we will overeat, or undereat, or swing backward and forward between the two extremes. The Buddha emphasized the middle way and this principle applies as much to eating as it does to anything else.

If we eat too much, food acts as a heavy weight in the body that blocks out any feeling of unhappiness and dulls the consciousness. When we experience anxiety or worry or even boredom, we find ourselves once again looking in the refrigerator or cupboard for something to eat.

How we feel often determines our actions. We can find ourselves going to the kitchen to eat something even when there is no reason except the fact that we feel a bit peckish. Sometimes we might experience a negative reaction toward food, and will virtually stop eating, although we keep thinking about food, our weight, and our body.

When we try to find a middle way between the two extremes we might feel empty, with a stream of unpleasant sensations in our stomach and the desire to put something in our mouth. Then the mind confuses these unpleasant sensations with hunger pangs, and we convince ourselves we need food, even though this may not be the case. We are misinterpreting the sensations as the need to eat.

It is important to remember that food and drink act as resources to nourish us in daily life. We have five senses, all of which nourish our life. All the senses matter equally, and sights, sounds, smells, and touch also provide a form of nourishment to our being. If

we are undernourished in these areas, we are more likely to run to the taste sense stimulated by eating and drinking and take something from the immediate world to fill us up and provide what we think as nourishment. We pay a heavy price for neglecting nourishment through the other sense doors.

It is important to see and hear things of beauty, to appreciate through our sense of smell and touch. We might observe the beautiful mandala of the rose, or listen to the sound of a bird whistling as it flies down and rests gently on a branch.

We may need to develop our sense of smell by stopping to appreciate flowers, incense, and perfume. Unfortunately the smell of food can make us feel hungry and we go from smell to a compelling need to eat. If we can develop an appreciation for the feeling of space within us, as well as appreciating the sensation of a good healthy meal, we will discover a wise, balanced relationship to food.

Sometimes it may be necessary to take ourselves away from temptation to help break the force of habit. In the Noble Eightfold Path, the Buddha emphasizes the *right effort* to avoid and overcome issues. If food is too close at hand, we may not have enough discipline to restrain the mind. Before we catch ourselves, we may be biting on chocolate or taking another drink. Maximizing time spent outdoors, regardless of the weather, contributes to nourishment through eyes and ears. If we really practice in these four areas, we will experience the benefits in our emotional life as well as the feeling of deep contentment in the body. It is well worth the effort.

One friend, a vegetarian, thought she ate the right food but could not stop her weight from ballooning. We discussed the matter together. She told me that she ate lots and lots of pasta and potatoes and little else. She resolved to start eating lots of salad before her meal instead of treating it as a side dish, and this had the desired effect. One small change can make a huge amount of difference.

EXERCISE

At the time of the Buddha, there were four primary forms of exercise—yoga, walking, building, and work on the land. The homeless wanderers who followed the Buddha spent nine months a year walking through the hills, valleys, and plains of India. This tradition carried on throughout much of Asia, but then began to decline as study and chanting in monasteries replaced the tradition.

My meditation teacher, Venerable Ajahn Dhammadaro of Thailand, walked throughout seventy provinces of Thailand as a wandering monk. For three months a year during the rainy season, the monks stayed in one place to practice meditation. Today, we have become a culture of extremes—busy and preoccupied at one end, and lazy and negligent at the other. Are you willing to include exercise in your daily life? The simplest form of exercise is walking. Walking a little faster enables the energy to flow much quicker. If you live in an area where there are hills, then walking up and down them strengthens the body, particularly the legs and back. Obviously, if you have any health problems then it is necessary to proceed with a course of exercise slowly and mindfully.

Some people never exercise, but are blessed with an unusually strong constitution enabling them to live a long and relatively healthy life. One 82-year-old told me that his only form of exercise was going upstairs to the toilet. He said without blinking an eyelid, "I never exercise, it's bad for your health." But it is important to acknowledge that such people are the exception, not the norm. There are many forms of invaluable exercise, some adopted from the Buddhist, Hindu, and Taoist meditation traditions of the East.

Regular exercise serves as a spiritual discipline as much as meditation and mindfulness practices do.

Old hands take gentle care of a young plant. Just as we plant seeds in the garden and tend them, so we plant seeds in the mind to develop our inner life.

PRACTICES FOR TODAY 2

1

Give ten minutes to gentle or firm exercise, according to your capacity

2

Bend, stretch, move the body, dance, swing the arms, stand up, let the head and back hang down—be imaginative in the exercise

3

Go outside, take a brisk walk, or do some gardening

4

Carry the shopping home with an even weight in each hand, rather than take the car

5

Make a commitment to regular exercise

POSTURE

There are two considerations that accompany exercise: breathing and posture. The Buddha recognized this when he said "go and sit cross-legged, with a straight back, and meditate." If we were to see our skeleton, we would probably be alarmed at some of the postures we adopt. Poor posture distorts the spine, creates pressure in various parts of the body, and leads to stress upon the organs.

As time goes by, the neglect of posture affects our total well-being. Our awareness of the importance of posture becomes clouded and we have to choose consciously to pay attention to posture, whether we are sitting at a desk in front of a computer, driving a car, or eating a meal. The sense of being upright enables us to feel alert, present, and steady in the face of immediate experience.

THE BREATH

We often take little interest in our breath, as it tends to be thought of as simply a function of the body that keeps us alive. Yet for 2,500 years the Buddhist tradition has recognized the significance of breathing exercises as a vehicle for a profound sense of well-being. The Buddha remarked that of all meditations, he regarded mindfulness of breathing as the most beneficial. He pointed out that it contributes to deep calmness, inner peace, insight, and awakening.

The daily practice of mindfulness of breathing—even for a few minutes—can make a genuine difference to our life. Even if we only remember to breathe in and out deeply in a relaxed way a few times a day, we will experience the benefit. For our own welfare, there is probably nothing more important than being genuinely centered and grounded in the here and now. This helps to keep our mind clear, our heart steady, and our body firm.

The breath is a tremendous support, rather like scaffolding for house building. Situations arise in life where we face great pressure from various

Sometimes, we may feel unwilling to go out due to weather or location. We need to know whether this unwillingness shows wisdom or fear—or both.

circumstances. One police inspector told me that he changed work, ended his relationship, and moved house in the space of a few weeks. Things were changing so rapidly in his life that he felt everything was getting out of control. He started experiencing panic attacks, palpitations in the heart, and fears about going crazy.

I told him that people who exercise control over others are often prone to the fear of situations getting out of control. Unless there is a focused and relaxed attitude, these waves of anxiety would continue—even when things ran smoothly. We made some agreements that he would:

❖ Remember to mindfully breathe in and out
❖ Reduce dependency on results
❖ Trust in intentions, even if misunderstood by others
❖ Create time to share his experiences with others
❖ Practice being in the here and now, since anxiety is invariably caused by thoughts of the future

I reminded the police inspector that he should practice all five as much as possible if he was to shake off the grip of anxiety. Patience is the key. In difficult circumstances, our capacity to bring our attention back to the breath can stabilize, even when we are facing the most trying moments. But this does not happen by itself; the capacity to respond in such a clear way comes with practice.

I recall a friend telling me how, as she walked home late one night in Vienna, Austria, she was attacked. A man grabbed her from behind and put a knife to her throat with the intention of stealing her handbag. She is a Buddhist meditation and yoga teacher and has given much time to practicing the mindfulness of breathing that is part of the Hindu tradition. She told me that as the man whispered his threats in her ear, she was able to remain calm and this allowed her breathing to stay calm also.

Then to her surprise out of her mouth came the words, "Do you think this is a good idea?" To her astonishment, her attacker said she was crazy and ran off. Although it is a rather touching and mildly humorous story, there is no guarantee that our capacity to stay steady under pressure will provide a means for protection. However, it is commonly acknowledged that when people show fear and anger, it can often serve to inflame greater levels of aggression in the attacker.

If we bring mindfulness of exercise, posture, and breathing into our life, we will feel more present, more in charge of our existence, and receptive to the needs and circumstances of others.

RELATIONSHIP TO HEALTH AND SICKNESS

Sometimes when we make a general overview of our physical circumstances, we experience various areas of concern:

❖ Loss of health
❖ Dealing with the aging process
❖ Loss of beauty or good looks

It is useful to be clear within ourselves about how much we are attached to health, youth, and physical appearance. If we are attached to them, we will experience anguish and concern around loss of health, aging, and loss of beauty. In matters of health, we endeavor to respond wisely to diet, exercise, posture, and general lifestyle, but that does not mean that we can safeguard ourselves entirely from sickness or pain. Circumstances can change alarmingly quickly through no fault of our own. Hereditary and genetic factors as well as accidents have a significant impact on our lives in ways that we could never have imagined.

In the winter of life, we are more in touch with its bare actualities. It takes acceptance to pass gracefully through the last period of our lives.

The basic elements are solidity, earth, air, heat, and water. We share these with the natural world, reminding us that we are part of it.

It is never easy to feel prepared for illness or accidents, and this makes it important to understand the interdependence of health and sickness. Some people experience worry and fears over the most minor ailment or sequence of unfamiliar physical sensations. The mind then runs riot, applying various emotionally charged labels to illness.

Due to the interdependence of mind and body, we can make ourselves feel ill through worrying about becoming ill. We should remember that no human being can sustain perfect health day in and day out. Periodically we have to accept sickness and pain as well as having to deal with other people's pain.

Do we have the inner resources to stay steady, no matter what difficulties the body is going through? A Buddhist verse states:

This body is not yours.
It does not belong to you.
It is not yourself.

This could be interpreted as a negative reaction or a reason for withdrawal from taking care of the body, but in fact it is a reminder that the body is formed out of nature, belongs to organic existence, and is to be treated respectfully, rather than as a personal possession. This perception of physical life contributes to nonattachment, enabling us to experience space around health and sickness issues. We can then put into perspective the change in circumstances of our physical life.

In Buddhist countries, people in the villages will say repeatedly, "Birth, Aging, Pain, and Death." It is a reminder that all sentient life experiences these changes—nobody is an exception. We need this kind of perspective and depth of clarity if we are going to stay steady when physical difficulties arise.

The Buddha said that those who develop lovingkindness toward others in their daily life will sleep free from nightmares. This makes it clear to us that practice plays an important part in our life, whether it is overcoming self-rejection, developing appreciation, eating a healthy diet, or sleeping well and contentedly.

May all beings be awakened and may all beings sleep well.

Meditation for Healing

Be in a comfortable posture whether sitting or reclining.

I am aware of the body as a living organism
I am aware of the body from head to toes
  as a collection of sensations, vibrations, and pulsations
Some of these sensations are comfortable,
  showing no sign of difficulty for my mind
Other sensations are unpleasant, uncomfortable, and
  painful
I want them to go away
  but they linger, changing from time to time
Let me not fight these painful sensations
Let me not put pressure on myself
Let me develop patience with the process
  for I have no choice in the matter
Let me remember to breathe when I need to remember
  to be even-minded
And even to smile at my helplessness
It is in circumstances like these that I must respond
  to what I can respond to and surrender to what I
  must surrender to

Meditation on Acceptance

If you are feeling restless, confused, or not knowing where to turn, try to slow down. Sit in a chair, straighten the back, keep the eyes open, and develop a practice of settling into the moment. If you are feeling too restless to sit in a chair, then walk up and down, indoors or outdoors, or let the body gently sway with both feet firmly on the ground.

May I breathe in and out mindfully three times to settle
  down
May I breathe in and out deeply to let the waves of
  agitation get less and less
May I accept that things do not always go as I would
  wish
May I accept that I am going through a hard time
May I accept that various impulses are arising from
  within
May I accept that they are arising to pass
May I accept that there are these difficulties
May I respond to the resources available at this time
May I find peace of mind soon
May I find the clarity that lies beneath these waves of
  unrest
May this meditation and my heart's wish contribute to
  the wisdom of acceptance

CHAPTER 3
Mindfulness of Materialism

Any material shape should be regarded as
This is not mine.
So that when material shape changes,
there arises for one neither suffering nor despair.

THE BUDDHA

We all know our part in exploiting the earth through the demand for consumer goods. Many people have too much already. Buddhist practices contribute to contentment with what is and bring awareness to right action. We learn to work with compulsive tendencies when shopping and bring more focus to a range of household tasks. Through such practices, we show respect for ourselves and for the earth. The Buddha encourages us to experience a nonpossessive relationship around material goods and allow for change in appearance, breakdown, or disappearance of items.

Remember that space, periods of silence, and stillness at home all contribute to inner peace. Inner calmness of being comes through developing mindfulness of the four postures. In Buddhist monasteries of meditation practice, much emphasis is given to sitting, walking, standing, and reclining. Care with each practice establishes a certain presence of mind and steadiness for the body. We can bring the same mindful presence to driving a car, for example, rather than making it a habitual activity.

At the end of this chapter, there are three meditations, *Lovingkindness Meditation, Meditation on Impermanence,* and *Meditation on Appreciative Joy.*

Leaving their shoes outside, Buddhist monks and nuns meditate together. In the West, there are more and more meditation groups.

People interested in Buddhist practice often ask me whether or not these ancient teachings are more suitable for monks and nuns living simply in monasteries rather than for today's society with its endless demands upon our lives as well as the demands we make upon ourselves.

I respond by saying that I have first-hand experience of both worlds. I spent six years as a Buddhist monk in rural Thailand and rural India, staying in monasteries and ashrams as well as an extended period in solitude in a cave. I am also a householder and parent in the West, with a home and modest mortgage to pay. I have as many personal, family, social, and global responsibilities as anyone else I know. I am also trying to establish the Dharma in the West for present and future generations by creating new teachers. If I felt that it was necessary for someone to become a Buddhist monk or nun in order for them to realize an enlightened life, I would not hesitate to recommend it strongly, but living wisely needs to take priority.

At the time of the Buddha, the people of India adhered strictly to the rigidity of caste. Sons and daughters followed in their parents' footsteps, and there was little choice or opportunity to break the mold. Yet, due to the effort and struggles of women and men, we have the extraordinary opportunity today to discover an enlightened way of living in the very heart of society rather than outside it.

The circumstances of our households may vary quite considerably. We may be living in a large house with lots of rooms, or in a small one-room apartment. We may share our home with others, such as family or friends, or we may live alone. We may or may not have pets. Whatever the circumstances of our home life, there are always a variety of household tasks that command our attention.

There is real satisfaction to be gained from a good spring clean and clear-out of every cupboard, drawer, and cabinet in the home, as well as disposing of unneeded furniture, wall hangings, and decorations. We can generate space by giving away unwanted household items to a local charity shop. It does not take much imagination to give a whole new appearance to a room without spending any money.

Resisting Consumerism

I remember visiting a friend in her parents' home in Sydney, Australia, shortly after I disrobed as a Buddhist monk. They showed me to the spare bedroom where I would sleep. I unpacked my bags and opened the wardrobe to hang up my coat and shirts. I pulled the wardrobe door a little hard as it was stiff and unfortunately the contents from one side of the wardrobe fell on top of me.

My friend's mother had 34 pairs of shoes, which were now in a big pile on the floor. I could barely see the difference between one pair of shoes and another. It was no easy task matching up the left shoe with the right one. Rather quietly, I put them back as best I could. The thought that kept arising in my mind was "What on earth could anyone want so many pairs of shoes for?"

Some of us may have a certain fascination with a particular item of clothing, and make regular trips to the local shopping mall to look for the latest fashions. To bring mindfulness to shopping, we need to consider what we have and what we use. We need to be willing to go through our home to see what appears truly superfluous in terms of practical and esthetic needs.

RENUNCIATION

Too many homes are cluttered up with too many things. Unfortunately, we have become so attached to numerous nonessentials that we cannot bear to pass them on. Then we start telling friends and family that our home is not big enough, that we need a bigger house to fit everything in. In most cases, the home is more than adequate but we have no space in it due to the sheer volume of consumer goods we own. We should not forget that the more we have, the greater the number of things there are to look after, the more to break down, and the more to clean.

The Buddhist tradition has wisely expressed the value of simplicity in living and renunciation. This does not mean we have to live the life of a Buddhist monk, but we can try to make a commitment to leading a moderate lifestyle, finding a balance between

From a Buddhist perspective, the home
reflects moderation and simplicity.

household items, art, and space, and developing a
genuine contentment with what is, rather than
indulging ourselves in the forlorn belief that bigger
or more is better.

Some of us may already live quite frugally, and do
not have the privilege of an accumulation of
consumer goods that can be given away. It is not easy
for us to feel inner contentment with what is, when
everybody around us seems to be thirsting and
planning to acquire more and more, and in some cases
succeeding in their acquisitions. Our society often
creates a sense of competition about material things
that can be very difficult to resist or ignore, for
ourselves and for our families, and especially for our
children. It is up to every one of us to look at our
relationship to what we have, and to have the capacity
to opt out of compulsive buying, only buying what
we feel we really need.

PERCEPTION

The Buddhist tradition makes frequent references to
the value of examining the forces of attraction and
aversion that affect the quality and direction of our
lives. At times, we find ourselves pulled in one
direction and then almost immediately pulled in the
other. Finding ourselves in the grip of aversion, we
hate doing various tasks, but this negative attitude of
mind affects the quality of what we do, often making
life unpleasant for ourselves and others.

One wealthy woman in London brought in the
interior designers to redecorate her home three
times in the space of a year, but still she could not
experience peace of mind. We forget that our
perceptions are influenced by our state of mind.
If the state of mind has a strong disposition toward
dissatisfaction, it will infiltrate our perceptions.
Then nothing is right.

*Taste in furnishings varies. Making people
feel at home matters more than decor.*

The Buddha says that we need to be aware of general appearance and details in our perceptions. Then we can respond wisely to what we perceive. He also reminds us that "in the seeing, there is just the seeing." If we remember this and keep it in our minds, we can safeguard ourselves from becoming judgmental, agitated, or upset about our home.

We might only see what we do not like or what is unfinished, and we cannot perceive those things just as they are—neither finished nor unfinished. We may need to tolerate some peeling paint, untidiness, and dishes left unwashed overnight. We do not have to get into a panic when somebody unexpectedly knocks on our front door—there is no point in running around frantically trying to make the sitting room as neat as possible. Let us welcome friends and visitors to our home and not be apologetic for a single moment about how the place looks. It is our home after all.

USING THE CAR

When driving a car, we should remember to sit upright in the seat with a straight back. Driving mindfully, we sit with our hands in the ten minutes to two o'clock position, while moving the hand mindfully to change gear, and always avoiding the use of the mobile phone.

More than fifty percent of cars on European roads are less than four years old. The car is now not just a utility to take us from A to B, but acts as a symbol of personal success. If we live wisely we will take a different view. We consider the importance of making things last, and the ecological consequences of consistently needing to stay up-to-date with the latest gimmicks featured in cars.

It is not unusual for some people to be thrifty in some areas and extravagant in others. For example, I know a woman who is very thrifty at home. She never throws any food away, and makes sure she reuses all her plastic and paper bags. She washes her dishcloths and hangs them on the line to dry so that they last for months. She remains very economical with her food, doing her shopping only from the local shops and supermarkets.

Yet, every August, without exception, she and her husband buy a brand new luxury car and trade in their one-year-old car from the previous year. She says that she and her husband like driving a new car and knowing that it has come straight out of the factory. She admits that it costs them a lot of money because of the depreciation of their one-year-old car.

A car can run for many years, if properly maintained. I believe we should seriously consider keeping the same car for seven to eight years to express our commitment to living in a sustainable world. There is nothing wrong in buying a new car or a nearly new vehicle, but it is important that we take good care of it, ensure it has a good lifespan, and only use it for making necessary journeys.

Some years ago, I decided to make a conscious effort to reduce the annual mileage on my old Toyota. I cut the mileage from ten thousand miles per year to six thousand miles per year. I decided to walk to the supermarket and use the train whenever possible. All of us can contribute to supporting a sustainable world, making things last, and saving ourselves money in the process. After that I decided to give up owning a car, even though I live in a small country town. Despite the inconvenience, it is a worthwhile experiment that saves money, supports the environment, and makes use of public transport.

We probably spend too much time and money on clothes. We could reduce our wardrobes and still dress well while living modestly.

PRACTICES FOR TODAY 1

1

In one room in your home sort out what you need and what you do not

2

Give what you do not need away to a charity shop or loved ones, rather than selling your belongings

3

See if you can develop more space in the room to relax the eyes

4

Sit in different places in the room to see the impact that these positions make upon you

5

Clear the room out mindfully rather than rushing through everything

SPACE

At home, three factors contribute to inner peace:

❖ Space

❖ Silence

❖ Stillness

Space matters to the eyes, silence matters to the ears, and stillness matters to the mind and body. Space enables items to stand out clearly, giving a feeling of room to breathe and move. It is worthwhile going from room to room and examining the sense of space. Simply changing the location of various objects can provide a sense of openness to the atmosphere, even if we are living in a small area. To do this, we walk into a room, stand very still and then slowly allow our eyes to wander over every part of the room. What would make the room more spacious? What would give a sense of harmony?

We often do not realize how much we have duplicated items in our home: kitchen utensils, books, cassettes, CDs, videos, and various gifts for which we have little use. If you look around your own home, it is likely that you will be able to identify duplication there. By creating space in our environment, we create space in our minds simultaneously. Over the centuries, the Zen tradition of Buddhism has developed a keen esthetic appreciation for harmony of form and space, and the inner benefits that it brings to our psyche.

When we have had a good clear-out at home, we often feel a genuine sense of relief and contentment. After renouncing so much, we can then sit back in the armchair and enjoy the moment of experiencing space. This quiet discipline helps us to keep harmony present in our home life.

When we clutter up our home with things, we also clutter up our mind. We have more items to think about, to worry over, and to clean.

SILENCE

It is not always easy to experience a deep love and appreciation for silence. Some of us find it hard to live with silence, and may have two or three televisions in our home that we keep on all day. Silence seems to remind us of isolation, separation from loved ones, and feelings of being alone. The television, radio, or CD player act almost like substitute friends, bringing relief from feelings of loneliness.

However, it is worthwhile for everyone to make time daily to experience silence. As we develop inwardly, our appreciation for silence grows, and sometimes we can experience an almost palpable silence that embraces our being. It is a certain quality of inner development that allows one to appreciate a totally silent atmosphere.

Some people keep a space in their home for meditation. The Buddhist tradition recommends meditation for both calmness and for insight. The Buddha says there are four types of people: .

❖ People who have both calm and insight
❖ People who are calm but lack insight
❖ People who have insight but lack calm
❖ People who have neither calm nor insight

If you have a spare room you could create a shrine room for yoga, meditation, and periods of quiet reflection. Otherwise use a corner of a room to keep a chair or meditation cushion to indicate a quiet, sacred space. It only takes a few minutes of silence every day to bring a meditative awareness into our lives. Our meditation room or our meditation corner can provide a helpful point of refuge, especially in a busy household. Try to set aside a period of twenty minutes or more every day for meditation. At the end of this chapter I have provided some practical meditation instructions that can be used regularly, whether we consider ourselves a religious person or not.

Mindfulness through all forms of meditative movement is essential to mental peace and inner calm.

MEDITATION POSTURES

There are four primary postures that we can use to develop inner calm and peace. If we consciously develop mindfulness in all four postures we will quickly learn the benefit and value of living centered lives. The principle of the four postures is very simple:

❖ When we sit we remain mindful that
we are sitting

❖ When we walk we remain mindful that
we are walking

❖ When we stand we remain mindful that
we are standing

❖ When we recline we remain mindful that
we are reclining

We spend far too much time daydreaming or thinking about what we have been doing or what we plan to do. The strong tendency to indulge in the past and future through countless thoughts weakens the stability and calmness of mind that are natural to it when living in the present moment.

STILLNESS

In the Indian tradition, it is said that Vishnu, the Creator of the World, goes to sleep at night. While asleep, he begins to dream and all of life makes up his dream. At times, it seems like we are living in a dream world, especially when energy, projections, and perceptions impact on each other and affect our usual reality. There are many ways in which our perceptions of events can alter our way of looking at things. Vishnu knows he is dreaming and he knows that we have the power to wake up from our dreamlike existence as well. In reality, our projections are a kind of dreamlike world that we can wake ourselves up from by practicing meditation.

We sometimes wake up in the middle of the night, and there is a stillness in the air that pervades everything around us, and a widespread sense of peace and contentment—all the problems of yesterday and the issues of tomorrow seem irrelevant. For once, we feel in touch with a bare reality before our mind gets

We often move between three levels of consciousness: deep sleep, the dream state, and the waking state.

49

Retreat centers provide the opportunity to experience the benefit of developing spiritual practices through the guidance of teachers.

caught up in a cycle of comparing, fantasizing, approving, and disapproving.

At home we sit in the chair and allow our body to be still. Our mind rests in the body, our brain cells stop chattering. Immediately we experience the stillness of what surrounds us. We take a slow mindful walk in the local park, and find a certain stillness amid the sights and sounds. We know the world around us as a peaceful place and that this perception of the world feels genuine. These moments of stillness are moments of meditation.

MEDITATION

In our daily lives, we seem to go from constant activity to sleep. We wake up in the morning and once again go back to the treadmill. Meditation offers a practical and helpful way to keep our hearts steady and our minds clear in our busy lives. More and more people in the West find themselves attracted to the Buddhist tradition for the major reason of meditation. There is no other tradition that offers such a comprehensive range of meditation methods and techniques to support our inner welfare. Meditation reminds us of the deep things in life, contributes to our spiritual awareness, and gives us access to deep experiences. As with many things that we want to learn, we have to be willing to apply time, energy, and practice to the process. Those who are willing to develop a meditation practice will experience the benefits and know they have an invaluable tool for daily life.

The most direct and powerful introduction to meditation is through participation in a retreat for a weekend or a week. You will receive all the basic instruction and develop the skills to sit, be still, stay awake, and be present in the here and now. If you do not have the opportunity to participate in a retreat or local meditation class, you can use books, tapes, and videos that give guidance on meditation. However, most people require a teacher to answer the many questions that arise so it is best to join a group or go on a retreat with a teacher.

THREE KINDS OF MEDITATION

In the West, there are primarily three kinds of meditations connected with the Buddhist tradition:

❖ Insight Meditation, known as Vipassana. This tradition largely excludes the religious features of Buddhism including rituals, worship, devotion to the guru, and the building of temples. It concentrates on the threefold training of ethics, meditation for calm and insight, and living with wisdom. It has become the tradition generally regarded as most suitable and applicable for Western secular life. This tradition also makes no attempt to convert people from their own beliefs.

❖ Zen Meditation. Zen Meditation carries some of the religious forms and rituals from the Far East. The student needs a Zen Master to point to the deeper truths of meditation. Zen Meditation maintains the strictest forms in the Buddhist tradition. It is a tradition rich in sublime rituals and poetic truths.

❖ Tibetan Mahayana Buddhism. Visualizations and mantras are often used. There is generally an extensive cosmology and a range of religious beliefs around merit-making, rebirth, heaven and hell realms, guru devotion, and achieving Buddhahood in the far-distant future.

Each tradition is suitable for different kinds of personalities, and each has many followers. Whichever tradition we choose, meditation in daily life requires regular, formal practice. We might think that meditation is getting to a particular level of consciousness or having a mystical experience. Perhaps we think meditation means stopping all thoughts completely, or making the mind empty. Some people think that meditation could be dangerous, and worry that they might go into a state of meditation when driving their car, thus losing contact with immediate reality.

PURPOSE OF MEDITATION

In Insight Meditation a moment of mindfulness is a moment of meditation. Meditation means developing the capacity to stay in touch with the here and now, to know ourselves, and to develop ways and means to work on the inner life. Through such meditation, we:

❖ reduce stress

❖ develop the ability to stay steady in the here and now

❖ learn to work with difficult states of mind

❖ practice being clear in the face of change

❖ open the heart

❖ realize freedom in the middle of all our responsibilities

The Buddha became enlightened while he was sitting under a tree beside a river.

51

We may experience in daily life a whole range of difficulties, known as *hindrances* in the Buddhist tradition. They are called hindrances because they obscure a clear and contented mind. There are five hindrances: greed, anger, boredom, restlessness, and doubt/fear. If you meditate regularly every week for say twenty minutes per session, you might become aware of the particular hindrances that arise most frequently for you. It is then a challenge to make sure that during the day there is the motivation to work on these hindrances.

For example, you notice that you get angry when you cannot get your own way. In meditation you find yourself caught up in an imagined dialogue with somebody else. Instead of being mindful of the breath while meditating, you are thinking about what you will say to this person and what this person's reply might be. This is nearly always a pointless mental activity since the other person has not read your script, and they will inevitably say something that you had not thought of and could not anticipate. Practice during the day means that you are committed to transforming your anger into wise attention and skillful responses because you are less interested in always trying to get your own way.

With the appropriate attitude, we are much more able to reduce the power of these negative states of mind. We are then able to make life easier for ourselves and for others too. When we are angry we burn up inside, feel unhappy, and others increasingly reject or misunderstand us. Lovingkindness meditations also can help us transform this negativity into deep friendship with those people we are finding it difficult to get on with.

PRACTICES FOR TODAY 2

1

Write a shopping list and take this with you when you go to the shops

2

Refuse to buy anything that is not on the list

3

Ignore desirable goods that you see

4

Practice walking firmly past items that catch your attention

5

Feel inwardly a certain independence from consumerism

We practice to make shopping a mindful exercise rather than giving way to impulse shopping only to find that we regret it later.

Men and women of spiritual practice love the night hours and the expanse of the night sky.

The same principle applies to the other four hindrances. Regular meditation practice will increase mental strength to work with an inner problem so that we can make changes rather than indulge in negativity. Otherwise we remain our own worst enemy.

Let us remember that every time we bring our wandering mind back to the present moment we connect with the immediate reality, with the here and now. We dissolve the unsettled mind of daydreams, fantasies, and endless thinking. We may have a wonderful meditation on one day and incredible resistance to it the next. A quiet persistence helps us treat unwelcome states of mind as a challenge. Practice is dedication to moment-to-moment mindfulness. Some people only want to meditate when all the chores and household tasks are over. If you wait for that, you may feel too tired with only enough energy left to flop in front of the television set and switch it on with the remote control. It is much better to leave chores undone while you still have some energy left

to meditate. We can also meditate outdoors on a summer's day in the back garden or a local park. The outdoors makes us more receptive to nature, and enables us to feel a connection with the sky and the earth—the intimate presence within everything is revealed to us. You only need to find a park bench and sit down on it with a straight back with your eyes open or closed. It is moment-to-moment mindfulness—just seeing, just listening, just sitting, just being a fully conscious human being.

Such experiences, both indoors and outdoors, can directly awaken us to important insights and understandings that may not have been realized if we had just sat mindlessly around in the garden or had only taken a casual stroll in the park. Meditation for insight can make a significant difference to our daily life if we are willing to put some time and energy into the practice.

We develop our practice to bring mindfulness to daily tasks (including driving), space, silence, stillness, the four postures, and meditation. To commit ourselves to maximizing our interest in and application to these mindful practices takes us a further step toward learning what it means to live wisely.

Lovingkindness Meditation

Be relaxed and comfortable. Close the eyes and access a warm, caring, loving heartfulness toward life. Be aware of the absence of ill will, and the desire to hurt or hate in the heart, so that you experience an authentic kindness and compassion toward one and all. Generate this warmth to those who are in the immediate vicinity and those who are far away. Develop this meditation so that kindness of the heart becomes firm and steady in you despite the many vicissitudes of existence.

We are all like leaves on the tree of existence in the spring, summer, autumn, or winter of our lives.

May my teachers, community, loved ones, friends, and contacts be free from suffering and pain

May my mother and father be free from suffering and pain

May my brothers and sisters and relatives be free from suffering and pain

May my children and grandchildren be free from suffering and pain

May people appreciate their interdependence on each other and the environment

May animals and creatures in the earth, on the ground, in the air, and under water live in safety and security

May I abide with a warm heart, clear mind, and be free from pain

May my daily activities through body, speech, heart, and mind contribute to the contentment, healing, and insight of others

May I find the resources for the welfare of others, and may I be willing to take risks for their well-being

May all beings know happiness

May all beings know love

May all beings be wisely supported

May all beings be free

May all beings experience awakening

Meditation on Impermanence

This is a formal meditation practice so that the understanding of impermanence runs deep into the mind. We practice to observe change, whether it is the breath coming and going, body sensations coming and going, or experiences and thoughts coming and going. It is a meditation practice of sustaining an awareness of change. We must be aware, however, that even the quality of mindfulness or awareness changes, and we must use this meditation to be as clear about impermanence as we can. This meditation reminds us that nothing is worth clinging to or being possessive about as everything changes.

I am mindful of the moment-to-moment changes of the body

I am mindful of the moment-to-moment changes in the mind

I am mindful of the moment-to-moment changes in the feelings

I am mindful of the changing painful sensations in the body

I am mindful of the changing painful experiences in the heart and mind

I am mindful of the changing pleasurable and neutral experiences

I am mindful of my existence that is subject to birth, aging, pain, and death

Seeing impermanence reminds me not to cling to anyone

Seeing impermanence reminds me not to grasp onto anyone

Seeing impermanence reminds me not to be possessive toward anyone or anything

Seeing impermanence reminds me to keep in touch with this unfolding world

Seeing impermanence reminds me that what arises will pass

To abide in freedom means not clinging, not grasping, not being possessive

May I live wisely in the face of impermanence

May I respond wisely to impermanence

Meditation on Appreciative Joy

There is much to appreciate in life
*   that touches a profound place of joy*
It would be a pity to ignore the daily miracles of
*   existence,*
To neglect access to appreciative joy
Even the sun arising in the morning is extraordinary,
*   the bursting forth of flowers and the journey of birds*
*   across the sky above the towns and fields, across the*
*   landscape*
Appreciative joy reveals through awe and wonder
Through children playing in the park and the
*   unexpected telephone call from an old friend*
We have much to be happy about,
much to marvel over
There is often much more in the inconsequentials than
*   in the consequential*
Let us stop still for a few moments so that we can
*   absorb the wonders of the moment indoors or*
*   outdoors, home or away*
Let us dwell upon the undying presence at the heart of
*   things, so our being knows the mystery at the root of*
*   our experience*
It does not take much to wake up
Only an extra commitment to our eyes and ears that
*   contributes to knowing the deeper intimacies of an*
*   excelled exposure to the nature of things*

Mindfulness of Past, Present, and Future

One understands as it actually is
with its possibilities and reasons,
the past, present, and future
and their liability to a ripening of actions.

THE BUDDHA

There are three fields of time—past, present, and future. Our perception of events matters more than we realize. The Buddha advises us to be vigilant in observing how "I" and "my" arises in terms of our concerns with past, present, and future. In this chapter, we develop a practice of learning to observe our mind's relationship to events.

For the Buddha, karma means the unsatisfactory influences of the past upon the present and the way those influences affect our intentions. The purpose of the Noble Eightfold Path and the practices is to bring to an end these unsatisfactory influences, such as emotional wounds, grief, aggression, selfishness, or fear.

The teachings remind us to practice grounding ourselves in the here, so that we learn to stay steady, facing the aging process with equanimity, rather than letting ourselves get caught up in worries about the future.

There are two meditations in this chapter, *Meditation on Naming the Suffering* and *Meditation on Equanimity*.

Sometimes we experience the painful influence of the past upon the present. We go about our daily life yet something keeps bothering us. Accumulated past conditions arise in the mind, making an impact upon the present. Consequently, we cannot find any real peace of mind. This unsatisfactory influence of patterns, and conditioning of the present by the past is called *karma* in Buddhist language. When *karma* reaches the present moment it is referred to as the *fruit of karma*.

A participant in one of my retreats told me she had been in a relationship for two years. She very much enjoyed the initial weeks of the relationship, but then she began to feel increasingly uncomfortable. Her partner had shown much warmth and kindness at first, but now kept finding fault with her. At times, he would get very angry with her for the slightest thing. She began to have more and more thoughts about getting out of the relationship, but then he would be very apologetic and tell her that he did not really mean what he said. Each time he said these words of apology, she would let the matter go and try to start afresh with the relationship but as time went by, he became more and more aggressive. She explained to him that she was beginning to feel afraid of him and

wanted to end the relationship and try to become friends with each other instead.

He took this very badly. He seemed unable and unwilling to accept that the relationship had finished, and telephoned her constantly, leaving numerous messages on her answer machine. Once he even stopped her in the street to demand that they meet and talk over everything once more.

These circumstances made it very difficult for her to find peace of mind. She felt that she was in a tunnel of darkness and she wondered how long it would be before she could recover her life and find peace of mind. This situation did not arise because the woman had done anything wrong, bad, or harmful. In fact, she told me that her main mistake was failing to listen to her own inner voice when she realized that it was telling her that this man had an unresolved possessive and negative streak in him.

It took her more than a year to feel that she had put the past firmly behind her. She refused to have any further contact with the man and was determined to stay physically and mentally free and independent of his influence. In Buddhist terms, it meant that she worked hard to exhaust the karma around this event. When we completely step out of an old situation, it feels like a heavy weight has been removed. There is a growing army of professionals in the field of psychology and psychotherapy, as well as other forms of mind/body work, to help people extinguish painful past karma, whether from childhood or adulthood.

THE PAST

There are two considerations with regard to the past. One is the actual event, the particular details, circumstances, and stories that we recall or in some cases have repressed. The other is our relationship to the past. We usually believe that our memory of the past is acting like a true mirror to events. This may not always be the case.

Our various thoughts and feelings about what happened can intensify the memory and the pain. It is not easy to distinguish between what actually was and our perception of what was. Past is past. There is nothing we can do in the present about the actualities of what has happened. However, we may need to turn our attention to past events to help come to terms with the experiences that we went through. There is

some risk, but it is a calculated risk. We may make the problems of the past seem bigger by focusing on them, and it may take some time to reach insight and understanding about the past so that we can lay to rest what happened and exhaust the karma. We can then turn our attention to the past without inflaming our emotions, memories, or thoughts. We have brought matters to a satisfactory conclusion. Through diligence and not clinging to the past, the woman knew when she moved out of the tunnel. She could then pass her ex-boyfriend on the street without the feelings of fear or anxiety.

Observing our relationship to the past means making a specific shift in our priorities. We are not concerned with what happened in the past, in the way we look at the past. There are a number of choices. For example, we may decide to see the past as the past so that we can cultivate a real sense of moving on

The Buddha reminds us to live like a bird on the wing that leaves no trace as it flies through the air.

Reminders of the past may bring joy or tears. We practice to be clear that the past is past.

PRACTICES FOR TODAY 1

1

Do you have an unresolved issue from the past?

2

If so, write it down, honestly, as you perceive it; take your time

3

Write it down as though someone else was writing about your intentions and attitude

4

How can you resolve the issue inwardly if the outer circumstances remain the same?

5

Write down and reflect on this response

from what was. We may think of the past and one particular situation as a genuine opportunity to learn about ourselves. We have to be clear about what we can learn from the experience so that the old karma is not reborn in our lives.

We might treat past circumstances in an impersonal way. This means relating to the events as a set of unwelcome conditions that arose and affected various lives, including ours. This acknowledges the various forces at work that influence the lives of others and ourselves. This perspective helps to reduce the tendency toward blame—either of others or oneself.

We can help heal karma through lovingkindness meditations. These reflections require a regular commitment rather than trying an approach once or twice and then giving up. It is a wonderful thing to come out of the painful karma of the past and to feel a natural freedom and joy in the present.

The Buddha has given simple and effective analogies to show what it is like to come out of the karma of the past. He compares it to someone who has been in prison for years and the day finally arrives on which they are set free. The Buddha asks us to imagine how that person must feel. He also compares the ending of karma with coming out of hospital after several months, or finally paying off a large debt. There is a wonderful feeling of relief that the shadow of the past is no longer cast over the light of the present.

CONCERNS WITH WHAT WAS

We could not possibly count the number and variety of experiences that we have had. We could say every sound, every feeling, every thought is a new experience. In the course of a single day countless numbers of impressions register upon our senses and they really are too numerous to count.

All of those accumulating impressions throughout our lives make up the past. Out of those impressions a modest number matter more than the rest. It is not easy to have a healthy relationship with all that has gone by in our life, but you can try to embrace all that has gone before. There are four statements that often arise about the past:

❖ what someone has done to me
❖ what someone has not done for me
❖ what I have done in the past
❖ what I have not done in the past

Unless there is wisdom, any of these four questions have the capacity to generate much pain and confusion in our mind. We then find ourselves caught up in any one of them, making our life in the present extremely difficult. Sometimes we know that we must practice to cut the train of thinking. Again, it is making a firm resolution not to indulge in any of them. We mindfully breathe in and out, or we walk for hours until we have exhausted the inner demons, or we write pages and pages expressing our determination to move from the past. Unless we can approach the particular issue in a clear and calmly reflective mood, we will need to resolve not to cling to the past. Otherwise, we build up all manner of unhealthy intentions and attitudes toward the issue, and these do nothing to help resolve it.

We have a healthy relationship with the past when we explore skillful means to examine the past, perhaps with the wise counsel of another or in a group. We use our imagination to develop new lines of approach. In these circumstances, wisdom includes returning to the past and regarding it as the raw material with which we can live skillfully in the present. Then we express a freedom of mind that helps us to distinguish what contributes to understanding the past and what sows confusion, if not turmoil. The Buddha wisely

told people to be aware of any indulgence in the past involving the self by asking the following questions:

What was I in the past?
How was I in the past?
Where was I in the past?
Who was I in the past?

The ability to examine the past and the ability to let go of it reveal the presence of wisdom in our lives.

Memories can fill our mind with nostalgia or blame and can act as a shadow over the present.

CONCERNS WITH WHAT MIGHT BE

The other important field of time is the future. The past has a personal history to it that serves as a reference point, but the future has no such thing unless we remain grounded in the present moment. We can project literally anything into the future. This sets up a major gap between the present and the future, between today and tomorrow, this year and next year. The self then produces more questions about what it will be in the near or distant future:

❖ What will I become in the future?
❖ Where will I be in the future?
❖ What will I do in the future?
❖ How will I deal with future situations?

Some of our latent tendencies produce waves of thinking about the future. The past enters into the present, influencing it and the strength of that movement generates projections about the future. It means that the past wants to give shape to the future, but that is often a very poor way.

When we feel insecure and unsettled in the present, we project into the future to escape from it. We tell ourselves that once we get through this period, things will get better. When we feel steady in the present, we experience clarity with regard to the future. This means that the present moment provides the key to understanding past, present, and future.

Usually we think that life goes from the past to the present to the future. It might be worthwhile approaching this in a different way. Everything comes out of the present. All our memories come out of the present. All future thoughts come out of the present. If we could begin to experience ourselves in this way, we would certainly feel much more grounded. Out of the here and now arise matters of past, present, and future. So we practice grounding ourselves deeply in the here and now, and develop this practice through taking much more interest in what we see, hear, and know in the present moment.

We spend far too much time thinking about the future—planning, planning, planning. Is the future used as an escape from the present, from taking responsibilities and connecting with what surrounds us in the moment? The future acts like a huge open space. Into it we can place our fears, hopes, grand plans, daydreams, and visions. Real or unreal, possible or impossible, this vast open space of the future makes everything possible.

We forget that the future reveals itself as an extension of the present. If we take care of today, tomorrow will take care of itself. If we live wisely today, then we will live wisely tomorrow; tomorrow resides in today. There is no substantial independent reality in the future since it emerges out of the raw material of today's events. Holding this mental construct lightly shows wisdom itself at work.

We take time out to go into open spaces to experience a different sense of things. We absorb the wonder of nature through our eyes and ears, and feel the air upon our body. All our appointments for the day are put aside and what we experience is an expansiveness and receptivity to the day. It is important to appreciate those experiences of joy, so that we can put into perspective our ambitious plans.

Time needs to be understood as a human construct. If we are willing to step outside this human construct, we will touch upon a different order of things that is remarkable, mystical, and deeply fulfilling. The Buddha has made it clear that time is a relative construct, suitable and useful in many situations but ultimately the nature of things is timeless. If we exaggerate the role of time, it denies us the opportunity to know the timeless nature of things that reveal so much joy and freedom.

BECOMING

The Buddha spoke of the process of *links of dependent arising*. He said that:

❖ From dependence on feelings arises desires
❖ From dependence on desires arises clinging
❖ From dependence on clinging arises becoming
❖ From dependence on becoming arises birth
(of the ego)

We often forget how many scientists, biologists, and philosophers have influenced our thinking, especially through education, economics, and politics. Influential leaders keep telling us that we live in a competitive world, and that we have to study and work hard if we are going to make anything of our lives. Society has adopted the view that our success as a human being depends upon becoming somebody in the future. As a result, we have created a society of winners and losers.

We seem to be in constant preparation to become somebody. Much of our schooling prepares us for taking on a role in society. As the years pass by, we achieve a certain position, hold it for a period of time, then inevitably the role fades away as we get older. In retirement, some people find themselves wondering why they struggled for so many years. They say if they had known then what they know now, they would have lived differently.

For others, circumstances work out well. They feel content with the outcome of their lives, but there may not be much depth to their experience. Others want to become something different from what they are. The desire to become somebody is often expressed through work, relationships, position in society, or success. In sickness, the desire may be the desire to become well. Such responses are very human, but Dharma teachings and practices encourage a deeper exploration of the experience of living.

We feel we will be better off through the process of becoming, but there is a self-deception in this. No matter what we become it will not necessarily make us any happier. In the workplace, the wish is for promotion, and success in this endeavor nearly always guarantees a larger salary. As a result, some people find that they indulge in extra spending, and use their credit card even more.

Greater income may invite substantial debts through loans for luxury goods or a bigger home. Material gain in the short term may run side by side with anxiety. Debts to the banks and significant standing orders going out every month easily place pressure on the inner life. We become better off only to become worse off. Examining the desire to become may help us to feel more at ease with what today offers rather than longing for the questionable promises of tomorrow. Some of us fear that if we do not work very hard to become successful we may end up poor, neglected, and living a life of passivity and indifference. Becoming springs from comparing past, present, and future. We put in so much effort to satisfy the driving force of the self.

Some of us work extremely hard in order to maintain our position in terms of what we have become or want to become. There is never time to relax, and no opportunity to enjoy the fruits of our labor. Nevertheless, we have the opportunity to experience more happiness than this; a depth of lovingkindness, and an extraordinary sense of participating fully in this great web of existence. To have this sense throughout our lives means making changes to open up the fields of perception. We do not have to engage in a massive upheaval in our life, but we need to stop, be still, meditate, and deepen our receptivity to today.

USE OF PRESENT TIME

Sometimes we need to laugh at ourselves and at the inconsistent beliefs that spellbind secular culture. One such belief concerns the use of time-saving tools. We have so many time-saving gadgets, including the car, the computer, the washing machine, the dishwasher, the vacuum cleaner, and the microwave. The corporations that manufacture these goods like to boast how fast and effective they are. Even something such as the remote control for our television or CD player saves us time in getting out of our chair to change the channel or volume.

Despite having access to all these time-saving gadgets, we seem to have less time than ever. By now, we should find that we have so much spare time on our hands that we do not know what to do with ourselves. In reality, we have become prisoners to time-saving gadgets. They have no power to create free time, and these machines offer only false promises. We rarely give ourselves the opportunity to truly experience the present moment, surrounded as we are by these gadgets.

We have schedules to keep, places to go, and a diary full of appointments. Some of us have other time pressures, such as a deadline for writing a book. Our

There is no better way to let your children know how much they are loved than by playing with them.

preoccupations with personal achievement, getting things done, and living as a workaholic become sustainable only at the expense of mindful eating, sleep, exercise, loving relationships, and contact with nature. There is a real cost to the quality of life when we become prisoners to deadlines.

There is no point in arriving punctually in front of our computer every morning if it means that we neglect our partner, children, friends, or the outdoors. The heart matters—far more than we think. So we have to address the two worlds in which we live. One is fixed in time, appointments, schedules, meetings at

certain times, and completion of tasks on agreed dates. The other world makes time secondary so that we are at ease with life. Heartfelt communication, play, walks, enjoyment, quiet times, creativity, and retreats contribute to a deeper inner world and an appreciation of the intimacies of life. It is all too easy to become attached to our daily timetable and disregard matters of the heart.

As parents, some of us overwork and neglect our children but there is no substitute for quality time with children and other loved ones. Some of us think that providing expensive gifts for our children, such as the latest computer game or designer clothes, will act as a substitute for attention, love, and quality time. You cannot say to a loved one or a child, "I have an appointment with you that will take ten minutes of my time." But that is in fact how some of us treat our own children.

It is not humanly possible to accomplish all the tasks that we set ourselves. We are human, not superhuman. It is a form of madness to add yet another task to our schedule and think that we can pull it off. The Buddhist tradition has wisely emphasized renunciation not only in terms of going from a householder's life to a monastic life, but also in acts of renunciation that express living wisely. What are we prepared to do?

It is a bold act to take steps to drop some activities that make up our daily life. If our thoughts or our friends tell us that our way of living has become

insane, then we need to sit up and take notice. That means dropping some of the things that we do, going through the pain of the loss so that we are reborn into a more spacious realm. The willingness to make changes in our life, and some of them radical, may be quite painful at first. Dependent on a busy and stress-filled life, we prefer the devil we know rather than making the leap into the unknown.

It is important to see the wisdom of making this shift from doing to nondoing, from less work to more play. Our mind may fight against this new condition of not being on the treadmill day in and day out, yet we will begin to love and enjoy life more despite possible cuts in salary, loss of opportunities for promotion, and loss of prestige among our peers. All that loss will seem worthwhile with our growing appreciation of living sanely and enjoying each day as it comes while contentedly going about our business.

Far too many office workers spend more time at work playing computer games than playing with their children at home.

PRACTICES FOR TODAY 2

1

Reflect on the significance of being
here and now

2

Is the present moment only an effect of the past
and cause for the future?

3

What makes you feel calm and steady in the present moment?

4

Bring the mind back to the present moment as often
as possible

5

Develop a larger sense of the present moment,
rather than just what you are doing

AGING AND DEATH

The Buddha says that birth, aging, pain, and death mutually support each other, and that we need to be clear that our physical life undergoes this process. There are no exceptions to this process, yet we do not have to feel imprisoned by this unfolding event. It is easy when we are young to act as if we will never grow old. It is very hard to think of being old. I remember my teenage daughter asking me, "What does it feel like to be as old as you?" In the pride of youth there is often much confidence, vitality, and exuberance. When young, we could miss a night's sleep and hardly notice it the next day. But time flows by, and youth, beauty, and health begin to change. We may not be prepared for these changes so there is resistance or denial of the aging process. We find ourselves looking in the mirror in the morning and noticing all the signs of aging, including graying hair, crow's feet, and dulling skin. We have probably put on weight as well, and experience a faster heartbeat when going up the stairs. We find old photographs of ourselves that we have not seen for years that remind us very directly of how much we have aged. It takes clarity of mind to stay steady with the moment-to-moment changes that highlight the aging process. There is no exception to it, whether one is rich or poor. No amount of cosmetics and plastic surgery will make the slightest difference to the aging process and to imagine otherwise is self-deception.

Superficially, this can appear to be an unwelcome situation to find ourselves in. We did not ask to be born, nor to undergo the aging process, yet we are all participating in it. The key to living at ease with aging is to be nonclinging—nonclinging to the present,

As we get older, there can still be joy and contentment with an inner life unmarked by circumstances.

nonclinging to the past, and also nonclinging to concerns about the future.

It means letting go of youth, beauty, and abundance of energy, and not clinging to ideas and projections of how we would like to be in the present. If we forget self-interest, we can actually stay steady and relaxed with the aging process. We hardly feel or notice any difference between one day and the next, yet we engage in a process that is changing our physical condition all the time. There is no resting place for it. To accept this bare fact of existence takes the problem out of aging if we remember to take care of our diet, posture, and exercise.

There is something of a wonder and mystery about the unfolding nature of life as it goes from one day to the next. Organic life passes through these great cycles of birth, aging, and death again and again in this vast field of existence. While mind and body support each other like two bundles of upright wheat in a field, the inner life can stay bright, beautiful, energetic, and vibrant throughout life.

VIEWS ABOUT DEATH

Not surprisingly, many people report that they do not feel their age. We often carry an image of what it must feel like to be twenty, thirty, forty, fifty, sixty, seventy, eighty, ninety, or one hundred years of age. However, there is a misunderstanding here. We are not the body, and we are not our age. We do not have to feel our age. The inner life can sustain much interest and vitality in every area of life, despite entering into the field of old age. We will not necessarily experience greater fear because we feel too young to die. If we live a full life, we need not fear death. We can experience the natural fullness of the day from today. Life and death both belong to that natural fullness. People fear death because they believe they have missed out or will miss out on something.

Reflecting wisely on death puts into perspective what we do in life. When we die we can take nothing with us. It is a simple truth to bear in mind.

There are circumstances where the natural deterioration of the cellular life of a person's body has a pronounced effect on the capacity of the mind. Even in such circumstances, it is often possible for a person to maintain a contented daily awareness without clinging to particular features of the mind that existed in the past.

There are four primary views with regard to death:

❖ Death means complete extinction. We live once, we die once, and that is it absolutely

❖ We are reborn or reincarnated in the great cycles of life

❖ When we die we will be born in heaven or hell according to our beliefs and actions

❖ We realize liberation. The world of change, of birth, and death has lost its hold over consciousness and we embrace life and death equally

Life is a journey full of the expected and the unexpected. We rarely know what is round the corner as we journey through existence.

These views may give comfort or discomfort when we approach the latter period of our life. It is not necessary to hold any of these four views, but it is important to see that the body is not the self, it does not belong to us, it belongs to nature. When we understand this well, it puts our life into perspective. You could imagine standing on the moon and looking down on the earth. You then zoom in on the continent where you are at present, the country that you are in and the town and section of the town where you reside, the street and the building where you live, and finally to yourself.

Taking this overview can help put our life into perspective with everything else in the vast web of existence. How easy it is to intensify our personal life through inflating the importance of our existence. To live with humility will help us to live and die calmly.

Meditation on Naming the Suffering

The Buddha says that the First Noble Truth is suffering, and it arises in daily life. Various types of problems arise, and we often keep ignoring them hoping, foolishly, that they will go away. We often do not realize how much we are under the influence of these problems, how frequently they arise in subtle and gross ways. This meditation serves to make what needs to be made clear as clear as possible. Give a week or even a month to name a particular difficulty that keeps arising in order to be clear about the frequency with which it arises. We may not find this meditation easy. It will be important to ensure that we are aware of what is not present (see *Meditation on Absence of* in chapter 8).

Here and now, I recognize that this problem is arising
I am aware of the impact it has been having on myself
*   due to its arising*
I am aware of the feelings, thoughts, and intentions that
*   form this state of mind*
I am aware of how easily the problem comes out
*   through what I say and do*
I am aware of the degree to which I identify with this
*   state of mind and justify it*
It not only makes life difficult for myself but also makes
*   life difficult for others*
Here and now I have the opportunity to work without
*   this state of mind*
Here and now I am practicing to let go of this
*   state of mind*

Here and now I am practicing to stop grasping onto this
  situation

Here and now I am practicing to observe that it is
  impermanent

Here and now I am practicing to observe that it is
  unsatisfactory

Here and now I am practicing to observe it as not me,
  not myself, not who I really am

I am aware that this state of mind is only arising
  to pass

I am aware that this state of mind is not worth
  clinging to

I am aware that this state of mind only comes from a
  similar state of mind in the past

Right now I have the opportunity to develop freedom
  from this state of mind

Right now I have the opportunity to see the emptiness of
  this state of mind

This opportunity is available to me here and now

Let me not waste this moment

*As parents, we often have to watch
our children take risks in the
process of growing up.*

Meditation on Equanimity

I have been hurt by what took place

The experience has left its pain and its wounds

There has been an anguish and distress over past events

I am not ready to forgive because of what happened

I cannot turn around my emotions that easily

Yet I do not want to keep burning up inside

That means that the past still dominates my present

So let me try to get on with my life today

Let me develop equanimity to what was in order to keep
  steady with what is

There is no reason to place pressure on myself to forgive

But I will keep the intention to move on from the past

To maximize my contact with the present

In time, I may come to forgive as a way of transcending
  the situation

It will show that the events no longer have control over
  my life

Then equanimity leading to forgiveness, if necessary,
  shows a true freedom of the heart

Mindfulness of Knowledge, Mindfulness of Work

Scheming (to deceive),
belittling and blindly pursuing gain with gain,
this is called wrong livelihood.

THE BUDDHA

The Buddhist tradition has taken the daily life issue of knowledge and work very seriously. It is worthwhile examining our intentions behind the pursuit of knowledge and developing right livelihood. We will find great satisfaction through work that nourishes us, as well as providing a worthwhile benefit to others and our environment. We may have to make sacrifices for this to happen, particularly in income.

This chapter reminds us that a well-integrated person experiences an alignment of their head with their heart, and of knowledge with caring feelings. We sometimes limit our perception of work almost exclusively to role, money, and time. This chapter explores work from several other aspects as well.

The Buddhist emphasis on right livelihood, rather than simply pursuing a career only for personal gain, attracts more and more interest among young people. It is never too late to make changes in our life.

The two meditations for this chapter are *Meditation on Service* and *Meditation on Not-Self*.

We live in a culture that rates knowledge as one of the highest features of human aspiration. Children from preschool to university spend thousands of hours engaged in the pursuit of knowledge. It does not stop with university as there are countless magazines, journals, books, cassettes, programs, and videos available for us to acquire even more knowledge. Now we have access to knowledge through the Internet, and pressing a few buttons on the computer enables us to access a vast reservoir of knowledge.

It is simply not possible to fill the mind up with everything that we want to know about, and it takes discipline to maintain wise attention in the pursuit of knowledge. There are some basic questions to ask ourselves if we have a love of knowledge:

❖ What do I need to know?
❖ What do I not need to know?
❖ Is the knowledge beneficial or a distraction?
❖ If the latter, what does it distract me from?
❖ What are the benefits in terms of the pursuit of knowledge?
❖ What are the limitations?

Often, we take an interest in one thing, move onto something else and then take up another interest. We start reading one book, get part of the way through it, then turn our attention to another book and start on that. We imagine that reading newspapers will keep us informed of events around the world and it is easy to forget that newspapers only touch the surface of issues.

Yesterday's news becomes old news and reporters quickly move onto something else or report additional new facts as they become available in a continuing news story. Reading newspapers or watching the evening television news serves as a form of entertainment. It keeps our mind occupied and what we read in the newspapers, what we listen to on the radio, and see on the television certainly helps shape our perceptions. Much of the time we take the majority view.

PRACTICAL KNOWLEDGE
The Buddhist tradition encourages us to examine our relationship to knowledge. There are things worth knowing about, but there also things that are not that important. The tradition reminds us to apply *discriminating wisdom*, otherwise we overload our mind with information.

Learning to Embrace Nature

I met with a professor of physics, who expressed concern to me about how much he experienced his mind wandering. He said that when he read an interesting book, prepared or gave a lecture, he felt quite focused. At other times, his mind wandered, even in casual conversations, while he was taking a walk, or driving his car. It had made him increasingly forgetful. I told him that he reminded me of the absent-minded professor syndrome.

The professor admitted that he had spent his whole adult life involved in intellectual pursuits, in the love of knowledge and thinking about new theories in physics. He admitted that outside his role as a professor, the world of sights and sounds held little interest for him. I left him with a choice. He either learned to develop greater interest in the here and now, or he continued to indulge in daydreams that kept him at a distance from immediate reality and out of touch with moment-to-moment existence.

The Dharma teachings remind us that there are important areas of knowledge that we must address if we wish to live with integrity and clarity. We have to focus our mind on certain priorities, so we need to know how to:

❖ Develop a right livelihood
❖ Practice basic ethics for a thoughtful way of life
❖ Work with personal problems
❖ Develop our mind to think clearly and to respond wisely to situations
❖ Meditate for calm and insight
❖ Develop lovingkindness and compassion
❖ Explore ways to enlighten our daily life

This kind of knowledge is a practical knowledge and suitable for everyone. The Buddha referred to it as the Dharma. If we concentrate our mind on learning and developing this kind of knowledge, it will put into perspective all our books, libraries, and Internet services.

If we spend too much time in intellectual pursuits, we get more and more out of touch with immediate reality. We have to find a balance between them.

Authentic knowledge touches us deeply so that we can respond appropriately to situations that affect our lives or the lives of others. There is a place for light reading and light entertainment but it seems a pity to lose ourselves in it. We do not have to be well educated to listen or read about matters profoundly important to our lives. Today, there is a wealth of information available for people who would never dream of picking up a sophisticated textbook on psychology or philosophy.

We can also listen to teachers who help us keep informed as well as use books, cassettes, and videos. The most powerful form for understanding still comes through direct listening and in that respect, nothing has changed in the past 2,500 years. We can know and understand more thoroughly listening to a forty-minute talk or having one brief dialogue with a realized spiritual teacher than reading a dozen of his

or her books. There is no real substitute for listening. Sometimes on a cold winter's night the last thing we want to do is to go out to listen to somebody give a talk, but it may well be worth the effort. Things may be said that have a real impact upon us, even to the extent of becoming a turning point in our lives. This is the power of direct human interaction.

THE ART OF READING

We may have the habit of getting caught up in the desire to read as much as possible as quickly as possible, which makes it difficult for a simple truth to reach our heart. It is only when words touch a deep place inside of us that they have the capacity to make a real difference. It is important to be willing to stop reading when a sentence, phrase, or theme has touched a responsive place within.

We could close the book for a few minutes. Sometimes just the simple act of walking up and down and reflecting on what touched us in our reading gives an opportunity to digest the insights. There are many lines of sublime poetry, and exquisite comments on human nature, including fiction as well as nonfiction, that have the potential to awaken our

PRACTICES FOR TODAY 1

1

Read one or two sections of this chapter
through again

2

Find in it a point that means something to you

3

See if you can apply it during the course of the day

4

Observe how you feel when you apply it

5

See if you can apply it on a regular basis

Newspapers are important in a free society, but although many people read them, few work for change.

lives. This requires unhurried, mindful, and meditative reading to absorb the deep truths available in the text. In the Buddhist tradition monks and nuns sometimes spent years contemplating a handful of verses, until they knew what they truly needed to know. That knowledge stayed with them until their dying breath, and enlightened their lives.

RIGHT LIVELIHOOD OR CAREER?

We often transfer the knowledge that we have acquired into work. Work is one of the central features of human life, and without it we would probably feel rather aimless. For years now we have been hearing about the great importance of getting our career together. Our political leaders keep telling us that the world is a very competitive place, and we have to work incredibly hard to succeed in a competitive society, both nationally and internationally. Career often seems to mean position, power, prestige, and a substantial salary with various perks to our personal advantage. It seems that if we do not subscribe to this view we are a failure, letting down our parents, our educators, and ourselves. We need to be bold enough to look again at our priorities.

In the Buddha's teachings of the Noble Eightfold Path, he refers to the importance of right livelihood. Right livelihood gives consideration to our motives, what we do, and the consequences of what we do. It also applies to the pursuit of study as we prepare to enter the workplace. In making the transition from knowledge to work, there are several important areas for reflection.

Right livelihood states that our relationship to others and our environment matters more than position and profit, and it is a radically different way of looking at the world. Fortunately there are many people in society who follow right livelihood. It is a credit to them that they keep faith with this kind of work, even though for many of them it will mean a lower income.

Others never think about right livelihood and seem totally absorbed in position and profit. Is it a noble calling, or are we trapped in the forces of selfish desire where making more for ourselves and our family takes priority over social and global needs? It is another profound area for questioning and not easy to take a brave stand upon, and it may lead to misunderstanding from others. It is not an exaggeration to say that right livelihood and the quality of life on earth for humanity and the environment are very much bound up together, and we can all make a difference.

The change from a career, with its emphasis on self-interest, income, and position, to an intentional commitment to right livelihood signals a radical shift that has far-reaching consequences. With right livelihood, we sit down and seriously consider every aspect of how we make a living. It means giving support through nonharming activities, so it excludes work involving:

❖ engagement in the research, production, and manufacture of weapons
❖ laboratory experiments on animals
❖ work in abattoirs
❖ destruction of rain forests
❖ the production of poisons
❖ employment by the tobacco industry
❖ dealing in harmful or illegal drugs

This means we must be willing to say "No" to certain forms of work and say "Yes" to forms of work that give support to life. There are some careers that seem to comply easily with the principles of right livelihood, such as teachers, doctors, nurses, social workers, and members of the clergy. However, important ethical questions still arise that require careful consideration and sensitivity, such as abortion and euthanasia.

FULFILLMENT AT WORK

These professions have an obvious social dimension to support others, but right livelihood extends further than that. There are many kinds of work that enter into a category that we might describe as neutral, where the job neither contributes to the sustaining of life or the destruction of it. Such work, indoors or outdoors, in the office or in the factory, requires an awareness of our relationship to the work:

❖ Is it fulfilling?

❖ If not, why not?

❖ What would make a difference?

❖ Do we feel our work is making a contribution
to society?

❖ What is our relationship with our colleagues like?

❖ Is there the opportunity to give support to
others in the workplace?

Our job itself may not directly help others, animals, or the environment, but nevertheless it will fall into the area of right livelihood if we bring pure motivation and love to the workplace.

The ego can easily feed on right livelihood as much as on career, and some people make a career out of right livelihood. They may pursue work in the nonprofit sector, such as working for charities and foundations, as a way to fulfill their personal ambitions at a later date in the profit sector.

Food reminds us of the web of interconnection between people. More and more people prefer organic food.

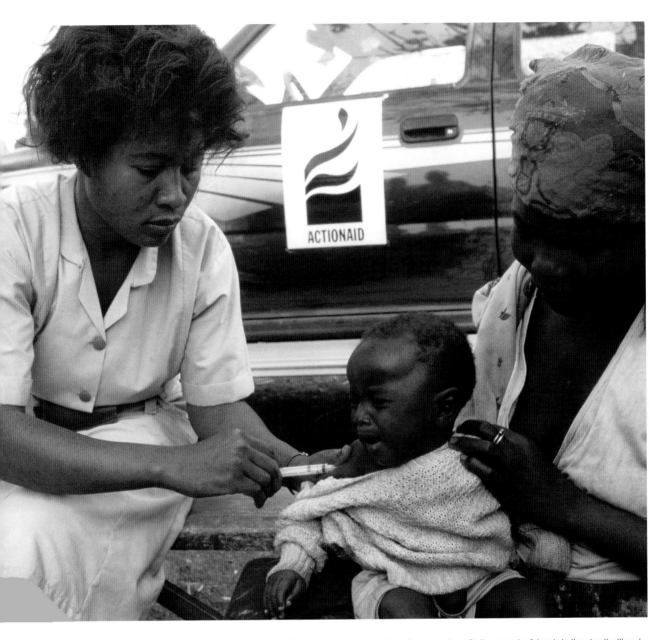

It is not unusual for people in everyday jobs to fantasize about finding meaningful and challenging livelihoods.

JOB SATISFACTION

We have probably all become familiar with the term "job satisfaction." For more than a century, workers have formed themselves into unions to challenge their bosses over wages, health, and safety in the workplace. Considerable steps have been taken throughout the last century in Western countries to ensure as much as possible that income, health, and safety are satisfactory for workers.

Yet there is still the question of lack of job satisfaction. Is the job itself problematic? Sometimes we think our job is the problem whereas it may be our resistance and negativity toward the job that is the real problem. If our attitude and quality of interest changed, then the job itself would appear different, but it can be hard to admit this to ourselves.

Sometimes employers refuse to admit that there is anything wrong with the atmosphere in the

Men and women can come together to develop spiritual exercises and practices that harness their focus and energy for worthwhile actions.

workplace, and place all the blame on their staff, or the other way around. It is not unusual for both employers and employees to be in a state of denial. Nobody is willing to take responsibility for the atmosphere that makes life difficult for everybody. When the atmosphere suffers because of the pressure to get things done, fresh ideas are required to bring the best out of the staff.

The Buddha placed immense importance on association with the *sangha*, which literally means "gathering" and refers to men and women meeting together to develop spiritual practices for enlightenment. There needs to be a sense of sangha in the work environment. Staff, including bosses, need to meet to share time together weekly outside of their day-to-day exchanges. Indoors or outdoors, office,

factory, department store, building site, or farm, there are opportunities to develop a sense of sangha. These may include:

❖ Meditation

❖ Exercise

❖ Yoga

❖ Group interaction

❖ Sharing experiences

❖ Stress-reduction practices

❖ Communication skills practices

❖ Inquiry into ethics, prestige, profits,
and environmental impact

We spend many years of our life at work. We may have an ordinary job, but we can bring awareness and a thoughtful attitude to every aspect of it.

It ought to be obvious to us that love of work provides job satisfaction. There is no substitute for it. Some people could not imagine working on the production line in a factory, or engaging in repetitive tasks such as cleaning in a hospital or running errands for a company. Yet somebody has to do such work, and everybody has a part to play. Bringing people together as a sangha can open the doors of wisdom through mutual understanding.

HOURS PER WEEK

If we are in good spirits and good humor on a daily basis, we create a wholesome, healthy, and nourishing atmosphere for everybody. Most people work more than forty hours per week and some work fifty, sixty, or seventy hours or more. We might ask ourselves,

"How do you do it?" If it is done under obligation or because of pressure from superiors, we may experience a strong reaction at a later date. Some people work long hours because they actually love what they are doing. It is often not so much a matter of how long we work, but the kind of connection we have with what we do.

We constantly tell each other how hard we work. In some countries people have only two weeks holiday a year to recover from fifty weeks of working long hours. Other countries offer their workers four or five weeks or more paid leave a year. It is not only inner change that is necessary but also social and political change to enable working people to live a more sane way of life and to feel a genuine respite from daily working life. Why do we work so hard?

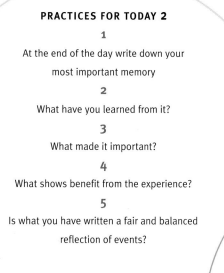

PRACTICES FOR TODAY 2

1

At the end of the day write down your
most important memory

2

What have you learned from it?

3

What made it important?

4

What shows benefit from the experience?

5

Is what you have written a fair and balanced
reflection of events?

*We can use a daily or weekly
journal to keep in touch with our
experiences and attitudes.*

What are the motives that are driving us along? There is very little point in complaining about the situation since it only tends to make the mind feel more negative. It may be necessary to make changes in ourselves and also support social and political changes. Often this can seem yet another thing to do when we are already working very hard just to make ends meet.

If we work less hard, we fear our own inner judgmental voice as well as the condemnation of others. They will think that we are not so committed and begin to question whether we are suitable for the role. Does fear drive us along? Are we afraid to make changes? We fear that we will not get the task completed, or that we will be rejected or misunderstood by others, we fear losing our job, or not succeeding at what we set ourselves to do. As this fear gets stronger, it begins to place an increasing amount of pressure on us, and the force of fear keeps rubbing up against the force of desire until there is a collision. In that collision we can find ourselves in a personal crisis.

Feeling rather trapped and anxious, we feel the heavy shadow of despair lurking above us. If our response to the question, "Am I working too hard?" is "Yes!" we will need to take practical steps to work less hard and to open up our inner life. When we cut back on our long-term habits, we may have to accept initially feelings of dissatisfaction and insecurity that may arise through this transition period. But no job is worth having a heart attack over and no job is worth neglecting loved ones for.

KEEPING A JOURNAL

Try to keep a journal of your experiences from one week to the next. Keep the journal beside your bed or on the breakfast table, or keep a small diary in your pocket. The purpose of a journal includes:

Stress and worry have become common features at work due to the inner collision between the desire to succeed and the fear of failure.

❖ To reflect on what matters

❖ To question fear and anger

❖ To see the wise alternatives

❖ To develop what needs to be developed

❖ To overcome what needs to be overcome

❖ To appreciate the beautiful moments of the day

❖ To acknowledge the most difficult moments
of the day

❖ To explore an enlightened attitude to
circumstances

To keep a journal properly, we must be completely honest. That means we neither exaggerate our responses to circumstances, justify, or deny them. What is our relationship to daily life? Are our relationships suffering? Are we feeling stressed? Are we happy? Can we acknowledge and express gratitude for nonproblematic times? Are we willing to write down our experiences without using emotive words such as *always*, *never*, *only*, *cannot*?

If we put all of this down on paper and read it aloud to ourselves, it may fire us up enough to find ways to discover an expansive life with a determination to stay awake in all circumstances.

STATUS, POSITION, PRODUCTİVITY, RESPONSIBILITY, POWER?

There is something almost magnetic about securing a certain status or position in society. We desperately want to become somebody. Some of us accelerate into areas of position and authority at a very early age. Intellectual knowledge enables bright, young minds to take remarkable leaps in authority in a short period of time. Some of us become dizzy with our new position, and we become conceited and too sure of ourselves. This conceit often acts as a mask to hide some underlying insecurity as we pay no respect to ourselves or others when we become impressed with ambitious striving out of self-interest.

*There is something very calming for
the mind when we have exposure to
an expanse of water.*

A very wealthy Asian businessman employed a trusted servant in his home. The businessman would always seek the advice of his loyal servant, even though the man had no education. It is in situations like this that we see that it is the wisdom that gives the authority, not having power. We ought to be impressed with people who express wisdom, clarity, and kindness. There is very little to learn from the conceited and ambitious, but there is much to learn from the wise.

The feeling of responsibility can at times weigh upon thoughtful and caring individuals, who question themselves on a daily basis:

❖ What have I done?

❖ What have I not done?

❖ What am I doing?

❖ What am I not doing?

❖ What have I got to do?

❖ What have I not got to do?

These are useful questions, but they do not have to be followed relentlessly to the point where they weigh heavily upon us. Perhaps we need to drop the word "responsibility" and replace it with "response-ability." This means the ability to respond wisely to situations without feeling the weight of them.

If we can hold our positions of authority lightly and steadfastly, we are less likely to abuse them through unskillful use of our power when our ego seeks immediate gratification. It takes deep awareness from within ourselves, and the willingness to encourage others to give us feedback, for us to keep to the way of wisdom.

Power is an agreement between those who give power to others and those who hold it. It should not be thought of as a personal right to have control over other people's lives, but a temporary agreement between people that helps to facilitate good relationships and mutual well-being. It means taking our areas of *response-ability* with a warm heart, clear mind, and the commitment to treat others as we wish to be treated.

A HUMBLE POSITION

Deeper aspects of religious teachings remind us of the wider context in which our life functions. If we have a deep sense of the greater whole, there is much less chance of our ego trying to grab the power and the glory for itself. With this sense of belonging to something bigger than ourselves, we can understand that we are in our position because of a variety of conditions that enabled events to happen. We are not really the commander-in-chief, nor in ultimate control, nor does everyone rely upon us. The world carries on with us and will carry on without us. There will be times when we find that events bring true humility to our position, and there is nothing for our ego to build up on so that we have to let go.

People enter a life of voluntary simplicity to maximize time for prayer, meditation, and service.

Accepting Death

I had a lovely meeting with a Catholic nun who told me of a passage in the New Testament spoken by Jesus that really affected her. She had become seriously ill for a period of time through cancer and her life contained a real measure of uncertainty. For years, like many people, she had swallowed the conventional Western dogma that we all have choices. After a number of tests, her physician told her that she had cancer. It seemed to make a mockery of her choices, past, present, and future. She then recalled the words of Jesus when he said in the face of his own death, "Thy will be done." Sometimes we seem to be only communicating to others around us our choices, our decisions, and our desires. It might be necessary at times to put all of that aside so that we connect with that unfolding of life that does not seem to have much to do with all our choices. "Thy will be done," said the wise rabbi from Nazareth. During this period of treatment, she said there was some uncertainty as to whether she would recover. She decided that before she died she would give away her possessions to the other nuns in the convent. She said then she started to make a good recovery from her treatment. "I had to go to the sisters and ask if I could have my things back," she laughed.

Meditation on Not-Self

May awareness observe clearly whenever the ego arises

May awareness observe clearly whenever the "I" arises

May awareness see clearly when the notion of "me" arises

May awareness see clearly when the notion of my arises

May I be free from trying to build up "my" sense of self

May I be free from putting down my sense of self so
     that I respond with wisdom to events rather than
     being trapped in reactions to the self

May inner awareness reveal a spaciousness around all
     events

May this awareness accommodate all I call my life

May this awareness see feelings as feelings, not as myself

May this awareness see thoughts as thoughts, not as
     myself

May this awareness see perceptions as perceptions, not as
     myself

May this awareness see states of mind as states of mind,
     not as myself

May this awareness see the condition of body as the
     condition of body, not as myself

So that wisdom abides in the face of the interaction of
     mind and body

Meditation on Service

I regard service as the noblest form of human activity

It means putting aside my own interests

So that I offer support to the world of others no matter
     what their circumstances

It will be a hard road, this road of service

There is no retirement from it

It signals the sign of a worthwhile life with the necessity
     to generate time for inner renewal as a mark of
     service for oneself

There is something noble about deep reflection
     that benefits others, that benefits animals and the
     earth itself.

I may not see the results in my lifetime so I have no
     need to look for them

Instead, I will rely upon the quality and commitment of
     the intention and make that the priority

Praise and blame may come for providing a service to
     others

Yet, I will quietly remain focused on the intention

Knowing that there is no wish to cause harm or
     suffering to others

CHAPTER 6
Mindfulness of Money and Shopping

It is called Nirvana because of the getting rid of craving for things.

THE BUDDHA

The Buddha points to finding the middle way between the two extremes of self-indulgence and self-hatred. He also points to a balanced and caring lifestyle. Such a lifestyle will reflect in our relationship to money and shopping. The Noble Eightfold Path includes right mindfulness and right effort. These two factors apply to shopping as much as anything else. Spiritual practice includes learning to handle our finances well, avoiding debt, and being conscious about the goods we buy, the materials we use, and developing an ethical awareness in such matters.

We do not have to be overly well informed in these matters. Often it is a matter of giving preference where possible to natural and organic products and not being caught up in the pursuit of fashion accessories. Unattached to the pursuit of goods, we find inner peace and can develop a heart rich in lovingkindness.

We can experience integrity when we shop mindfully, rather than becoming pushed and pulled around on sudden whims. Part of the practice is learning to make things last.

The two meditations for this chapter are *Contentment with What Is* and *Lovingkindness Meditation*.

In the Buddhist tradition, there are two guidelines for those wishing to become a Buddhist monk or nun. Firstly, permission is required for ordination from a close family member. For example, if a man is married, he must have permission from his wife; otherwise he might become a monk as a way of fleeing from personal responsibilities.

The second rule for ordination concerns money. A man or woman cannot take ordination unless he or she is free of debt, as the monastic life can hold an attraction for those who have to pay off personal loans. We are often not aware of the impact that debt has upon us, but it can easily become a source of anxiety as the mind thinks endlessly about the burden of the debt. There are five types of personal debt:

❖ Debts born from student loans
❖ Debts born from the purchase of consumer goods, whether in the long or short term
❖ Debts from gambling, including on the stock exchange
❖ Debts born from a mortgage
❖ Debts born from a loan from the bank, loan company, family member, or friend

Education is a passport to income. We need to learn to handle finances wisely.

We see that all five areas matter equally, otherwise our perceptions around money become distorted through fear and greed. For example, student loans in the USA can run from a few thousand dollars to a hundred thousand dollars. It seems a harsh system that demands that students go into debt and then have to work incredibly hard in the public or private sector to pay off these loans. Students in debt find themselves in the grip of bonded labor not so different from the bonded labor of the Middle Ages.

The harsh reality shows that students hardly have any choice if they wish to enter the work force. They may feel that there is no escape from the debt, and the bondage continues for many years. It is important to keep as clear a mind as possible, with a steady

It is easy to get ready cash these days, but pleasure can turn to pain through compulsive shopping.

intention to pay off such loans systematically. Money also has an emotional factor and the interaction of the self with money can provoke all manner of fears.

HANDLING MONEY

Some of us think and speak in very emotive language when money issues arise. We are plagued by fears of becoming a beggar with little to eat and no roof over our head. It is very unlikely that such desperate circumstances would arise, but the fear says otherwise. You must be mindful about money issues, and this will help you put financial matters into perspective.

Intense attachment to money sets families against each other, creating discord and conflict. Money, desire, and the self become entangled, producing intense greed and envy. Everybody involved thinks they are right and everybody else is wrong and lawyers are often hired to resolve the situation.

Wealth and Unhappiness

The family was wealthy. The father had run a successful business for years and had retired. Three of the children lived overseas while the other child stayed to take care of the family business. The parents had said for many years that they would divide their assets equally between all four children when they died. The son who helped in the family business disagreed since he had stayed behind, and felt his brothers and sisters should have a much smaller percentage. The parents said the son did not need a larger percentage since he had become independently wealthy, but the son said it was the principle that mattered. The money issue became a source of conflict that went on for years. The conflict brought division to the family and grief to the parents. It is not an uncommon story.

Many of us simply do not know how to handle money well. Day in and day out, we face endless temptations to spend money. Debts can accumulate, even though it might be a relatively simple matter such as a telephone bill. The bill can grow and grow if we allow ourselves to forget that ultimately it will have to be paid. Big debts or small debts can play havoc with the mind unless we bring mindfulness and clear comprehension to money matters.

Despite all the business studies courses now offered in schools, there is little emphasis on learning to handle our own financial affairs. How many students, for example, discuss openly in the classroom their bank account, their monthly allowances, how they spend their money, and how much money they regularly save, if any?

PERSONAL FINANCE

Money is still a major taboo in society, and this is evident in our reluctance to tell others how much we actually have, or how much we are in debt. In this private world of personal finances, we are left to sort out our money matters for ourselves or with our personal accountant. To handle money matters well, we must first acknowledge that money is emotional as well as rational. We can consider:

> ❖ Who can I talk to that I trust about my
> money issues?
> ❖ When am I vulnerable to impulses?
> ❖ What do I need to practice to renounce?
> ❖ What brings me joy that money cannot buy?
> ❖ Can I sit down and write out my finances
> without denial, fear, or optimism?

We may need to develop a fresh relationship to money so that we become aware that money is only one feature in the web of life, and not the spider itself. We have to break ourselves out of the stranglehold of thinking of ourselves as consumers, even having the courage to be downwardly mobile instead of upwardly mobile. If we are fortunate enough to have investments, we need to be well informed about how our money is used by others and reflect on the ethical considerations this raises.

Most religions emphasize the importance of faith in God as a means of transcending worldly problems; we have tried to make ourselves into mini-Gods through money and property. The Buddha made a shift away

from this viewpoint by placing mindfulness of issues at the center of life. He frequently used the word *samadhi* to support mindfulness. Samadhi is a meditative concentration enabling the mind to stay firm and steady in the face of issues. Our relationship to money need be no different to our relationship to anything else—calm and clear or distressed and agitated.

Samadhi expresses a power of mind to strip away all our projections that make a fetish of money, and to see such matters in context. On one level, money consists of numbers on pieces of paper. Those numbers may be black or red, or moving backward or forward between the two, but it is unsatisfactory to owe money and equally unsatisfactory to be owed money. Two of the forces that the Buddha gave much attention to, namely desire and anger, often lurk in the recesses of the mind if we remain attached to always getting our own way in money matters.

The practice of samadhi helps us get back to basics, and stay focused, cutting the stranglehold that greed and anger have over us. Practicing to keep steady with this bare truth in a skillful way helps us handle money matters free from fear and impulsive expenditure.

TAKING RISKS

If we are having problems with money, we should not keep it secret but should take steps quickly to help develop a clear and practical relationship to our finances. If we have a debt, we may have to think in the long term about clearing it. There is no substitute for a quiet, systematic approach that will enable us to work conscientiously to clear the loan over a period of time. That does not mean that we have to make it the absolute priority, but we should remember that it would be foolhardy to increase the debt.

There are countless stories of people who have taken large risks and as a result have made a lot of money. This often involves taking out a substantial loan from the bank, and risking their home. Investing their money in a business project, they find the wheels of fortune turn in their favor and they become wealthy as a result. "You can be anything you want to be" is a popular mantra in Western society.

It is easy to forget the many businesses that fail. One woman, preparing to open her first restaurant, found the pressure very intense. She feared that customers would not like her menu and that the place would flounder within the first few months. She experienced so much stress that for a week before the official opening of the restaurant, she found that she could not even get out of bed during the day. She was forced by this to leave everything to her business partner, who then attended alone to all the details in the week before the opening.

All of her fears were ungrounded. The restaurant was a great success. Two years after it opened, it received an award from a magazine. This is an example of a painful state of mind trapped in fears of failure with no foundation. The discipline of meditative concentration trains the mind to take care of one day at a time, and this safeguards the mind from getting caught up in projections about the future. The Buddha said: "Mind is the chief. Mind is the forerunner."

A spider's web reminds us of the way every feature of life links to everything else. As we cultivate awareness, we see this interconnection.

KEEPING A RECORD

All this does not mean to say that we should never take risks. We need to approach business ventures wisely and clearly without rushing into decisions. When entering into any kind of financial partnership with someone else, we need to feel a genuine sense of trust and confidence with that person. However, important agreements must always be put in writing. Minutes of meetings should be safely kept to keep an accurate record, even among the best of friends or family members.

The Buddhist tradition reminds us in an unfailing way about the importance of impermanence, change, and discontinuity. Events can unfold in ways that we never imagined. This applies in our relationships to others in business and work activities as much as in our personal relationships. What is on paper matters more than the way the mind remembers it. Paying attention to the record can safeguard us from waves of anxiety and distress. We may make decisions that in the light of fresh knowledge we would not have made.

The practice of samadhi—keeping the mind steady in the face of change—is important here also.

It is all too easy to rush into something on a wave of emotional enthusiasm only to find that days or years later we bitterly regret the steps we took. Our mettle is proved in our relationship to such circumstances. Let us never forget that a calculated risk is still a risk. A risk means that we are prepared to let the outcome be in the hands of others, or be as a result of circumstances beyond our control.

FINANCIAL DEPENDENCY ON OTHERS

One retreatant told me that she did not have much money while her partner was quite well off, with a substantial income from his job. She told me that he always wanted to pay for everything, including airline

We have a responsibility to both present and future generations. We need to remember this responsibility.

tickets, holidays, meals in restaurants, even buying her clothes for her. As time has gone by, she felt more and more financially dependent upon him. Although he remained very relaxed about the arrangement, she felt uneasy about being in such a situation. At times, she experienced negativity toward herself for this dependency, even though he could easily afford to cover both their costs.

She asked me what she should do about the situation. After asking her a few more questions, I told her that there are times when we need the capacity to receive as much as we need the capacity to give. I suggested that her partner needs to be genuinely at ease with giving, and she must remain at ease with receiving. She should be sure that there will be no backlash later on if the relationship ends. There are many ways to offer kindness. Money is only one form. Think of different forms of kindness you can offer to him.

There is nothing inherently wrong with being the beneficiary of another's generosity as long as the two people involved act in a clear and wise way at all times. To ensure this, it might be necessary to check in with each other once a month so that both remain clear and comfortable with the agreement. It is the agreement that counts,

not the sums of money involved. The same principle also applies to parents, though this can be a more emotionally charged situation. Sometimes children who remain dependent on their parents well into adult life find themselves hearing another of Western society's most popular mantras: "All that I have done for you..." As parents, some of us give money to our children with strings attached, such as expectations of them to fit in with our wishes.

Some of us try to keep control over our children's lives through financial support. Children who have entered into adulthood may have to reflect on the possible consequences of financial dependency upon their parents, as it can become a breeding ground for resentment, fear, and guilt.

Some of us want to help our children in their studies or to get them established in the workplace

PRACTICES FOR TODAY 1

1

Examine your financial situation,
its inflow and outflows

2

Do you put money aside to support
worthwhile causes?

3

Find a way today to show an act of generosity

4

Do not tell others; there is a kind of inner power
in anonymous gesture

5

Remember that to give expresses
a freedom of spirit

*Parents set an example
to children when
making donations to
charitable causes.*

and we might be able to pay for their support or make a loan over a period of time. These agreements need to be as clear as possible from the outset. Everything needs to be written down to clarify the nature of the agreement and the intentions and purpose behind it.

INSECURITY

Over the years, I have listened to too many heart-breaking stories of families and partners living together and getting themselves into nightmare situations because of conflicts with money. Acts of generosity and genuine gestures of goodwill become sour and this can lead to a life of living hell for those unfortunate enough to be involved.

It seems sometimes that the old proverb "money is the root of all evil" is true. Obviously, it is not money *per se* that is the problem, but the misunderstanding and attachment to it that generates the confusion. Money is highly emotionally charged, and it is important for us to examine these emotions in relation to financial matters. Pleasant or unpleasant emotions can result in desire, attachment, and clinging to unnecessary things.

As we dig deeper into ourselves, we sometimes experience waves of insecurity that attach themselves to money matters. For example, when we are travelling we might carry our money and credit cards with us in our wallet, purse, or money pouch, which we are then unable to find: we can't find it on our body, nor in our bag, nor is it visible in our room. A whole wave of fearful emotion rushes through us. Until that moment, we had no idea how quickly we had become identified with the money. However, if we develop a practice of inner security through stabilizing our heart life in our day-to-day life, we can bring a degree of steadiness to the presence and absence of money, either in the short or long term.

GIVING

It is a difficult thing to live feeling secure, unconcerned about having or not having enough money. We cultivate nonattachment while remaining down-to-earth in day-to-day matters. There is something skillful in having a fluid relationship around financial matters, avoiding the extremes of, on the one hand, being stingy, tight, and fearful, and on the other hand, giving everything away in grandiose gestures. I have witnessed many tears from religious devotees who gave away their savings or their inheritance to a guru or expanding religious empire only to realize later they had been duped.

I remember one woman who sold her apartment in London, donated all the proceeds to her guru in his ashram in India so that she could spend the rest of her life in a small room in his large ashram to be near him. Within a week of her giving all of her money to the ashram, the guru and his group of personal attendants vacated the Indian ashram and went to live in America to start a huge center there.

It left her in deep distress with a room in an ashram that had largely been deserted. It took her a long time to get over the situation. Eventually she returned to the West to rent a small room in a poor district of the city. It gave her no comfort when devotees of the guru told her it was her karma.

It is not only important to be able to receive money wisely, but it is also important to be able to give money wisely as well. We need to know ourselves, our intentions, and to also have trust and confidence in the beneficiaries of our acts of kindness. If we can keep our hearts and minds clear, we have the opportunity to live at peace with ourselves and at peace with others.

It is a blessing to receive gifts from others, but it is a noble person that gives without expectation of return. Even if we live our lives on a tight budget, we can nearly always find some money to give to support others who are less fortunate than ourselves. Giving is a practical way of reminding ourselves that we live in an interconnected world.

Others often have great need of our time, energy, and support. We can also give to others through making time for them in our busy lives. Followers of the Buddha were once living in huts together when one of them became sick with dysentery, but nobody was attending to him. The Buddha said to everyone: "Here you have neither mother or father to look after you. If you do not look after each other, who will look after you? Let him who would look after me, look after the one who is sick."

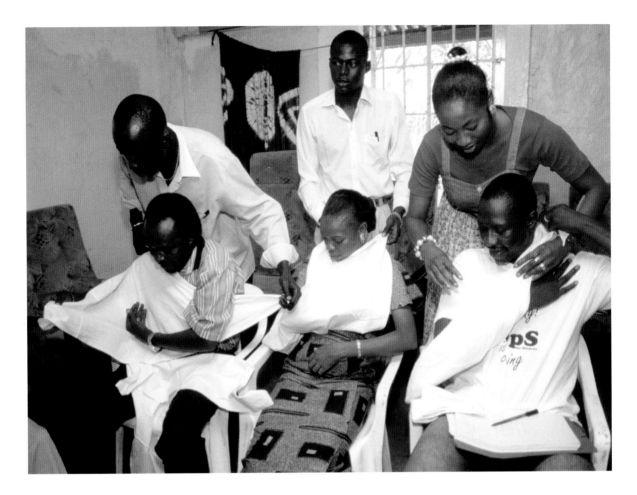

There are various ways we can give to others. These include giving love, time, skills, support, energy, and money.

Governments cannot legislate for kindness and generosity: that comes from the heart. Let us give time and practical support to others regularly as a deep expression of our acknowledgment of people, animals, and the environment.

SHOPPING

Sometimes it seems that shopping bears a relationship to the time when human beings lived as hunter-gatherers in the prefarming era. In a survey, teenage women were asked what they liked doing most. The reply from the great majority was "going shopping." It is worthwhile becoming well informed prior to going shopping because doing so will enable us to shop with discernment so we can:

❖ Support companies and goods that benefit people, animals, and the environment and avoid as much as possible those companies and goods that neglect such considerations

❖ Avoid luxury goods and support moderation in your lifestyle

❖ Buy natural cotton rather than synthetic materials

❖ Buy items that will last and recycle items wherever possible

❖ Do not cling to a fixed image of exactly what you want to buy

❖ Let go of language such as "I just wanted to spoil myself today"

❖ Keep as close as possible to the items that you need rather than impulse buys

❖ Take no notice of your projection onto an item that says "buy me, buy me"

❖ Buy presents that have merit to them

all too easy to go out and buy things that we really do not need. I met with one young advertising executive who told me that he spent several hundred pounds every month on clothes. He said at times he would even buy items that were too small for him to show himself that he could afford to buy them.

The "live now, pay later" philosophy often means short-term pleasure, and the bill usually arrives after the pleasure has been exhausted. The most noted period for intense shopping occurs during the weeks leading up to Christmas. There is a frenzy of buying that people enter into with unquestioning obedience. Countless sums of money get spent on goods for friends and relatives that they do not want, do not need, and would never dream of purchasing themselves. Of course they will say quite the opposite.

Shopping requires a wise discernment rather than submitting to urges to shop, shop, shop.

PRACTICES FOR TODAY 2

1
Is there anything in your home that you would like to change?

2
If so, go to it—for example, furniture, clothes, wall paint—and practice being content with what is present

3
Make today a day for not adding anything more to your possessions, except basic food items

4
Practice feeling at home with what you have already

5
Reflect on the value of not craving things

Without realizing that it is happening, we may develop envy of people who are better off, when we go window shopping.

96

THE FORCE OF DESIRE

The Buddha made it clear that he offers householders a different model for a sane life that gives equal consideration to both inner work and outer work. Without this wisdom, we will find ourselves repeatedly submitting to our desires and tendencies to grasp for things for the sake of a brief, pleasurable sensation. As parents we make large sacrifices for our children, yet we find ourselves unable to fend off the pressures that are on our children to join in with the consumer culture.

We need to pass on to our children and other people's children the value of a happy, playful, and inexpensive upbringing and resist the corporate world that has targeted young people, including children, to get the money from their parents to buy clothes, toys, and computer accessories.

Business has created a climate where children often decide that they really want something. As parents we may not want to spend so much money on a particular item of clothing, or game or toy, but children can be remarkably persistent. They know that if they keep the pressure up, we will probably give in after a period of time.

There is no simple answer to dealing with questions of desire, either our own, others', or our children's. We have an important word in the English language: "no." If we say "no," then we must mean it and make clear to others and ourselves the reason for it. When we say "no" to desire, we must back it up with the full authority of the mind.

In considering desire it is worthwhile memorizing the Four Noble Truths:

❖ There is suffering
❖ Desire is a cause of suffering
❖ There is release from the causes of suffering
❖ The practice of the Noble Eightfold Path
will end suffering

Association with wise and humble monks and nuns can help us find balance and harmony in our lives.

Children in the developing nations seem content with little; they also seem willing to take care of their younger brothers and sisters. These children will feel lucky if they have a single toy to play with, such as a ball or a small metal wheel and a stick to hit it with to keep it upright along the streets. Western children certainly do not seem happier for having their rooms overflowing with various toys. Parents have to find the middle way between harsh austerity and willful indulgence. Mindfulness needs to be at the foreground to ensure that any purchases are practical, sustainable, and nonharmful.

At times like these, it seems very hard to get governments in a capitalist society to redistribute the wealth more evenly to help the world's poor and genuinely protect our environment, so there's no point in waiting around for government legislation. We have to start making changes among ourselves so that expressions of compassion take place at the personal, social, and global level, as well as actively supporting organizations for a sustainable world.

Meditation on Contentment with What Is

We can practice this meditation anywhere and at any time. If we only give two or three minutes to this meditation on a regular basis, we can experience contentment with the way things are. It will help us to understand that simply getting our own way, or successfully getting what we want, never ensures contentment of mind.

There is nothing that I want from the world
There is nothing that will bring me contentment
I do not have to add more goods to what surrounds me
I practice to make things last
I practice to appreciate what I have already
I practice to let go of my impulses

I practice to support a sustainable world
I practice to show that I care for others
I practice to show I am already full and complete
When I pursue more for myself
I lose access to what is outside of myself
When I pursue more for myself
I become demanding and frustrated
When I pursue more for myself
I throw away the opportunity for contentment
I throw away the opportunity for peace of mind
I breathe in and out through this desire
There is enjoyment to be found in what is available
*   already*
There is contentment in letting impulses go
There is peace here and now
When desire collapses through lack of support

Light and color permeates the day.
Natural joy matters more than the
pursuit of pleasurable sensations.

Three horses enjoy a brisk gallop. The way we treat animals reveals our lovingkindness to such creatures.

Meditation on Lovingkindness

Be relaxed and comfortable, close the eyes, and access a warm, caring heartfulness. Be aware of the absence of any form of ill will in the heart. Generate this friendship to anyone who is in the immediate vicinity, including yourself. Then direct the meditation far and wide. Develop the meditation so that kindness and deep friendship become firm and steady, despite the vicissitudes of daily life.

May my mother and father be free from suffering and pain

May my brothers and sisters and relatives be free from suffering and pain

May my children and grandchildren be free from suffering and pain

May my teachers, loved ones, and associates be free from suffering and pain

May people appreciate their interdependence on each other and the environment

May animals and creatures in the earth, on the ground, in the air, and under water live in safety and security

May I abide with a warm heart, clear mind, and be free from pain

May people and creatures everywhere be happy and content

May my daily activities through body, speech, and mind contribute to the contentment, healing, and welfare of others

May I find the resources to be of benefit to others

May I be willing to take risks for their well-being

May all beings know happiness

May all beings know love

May all beings be wisely supported

May all beings be free

May all beings experience awakening

Mindfulness of the Powers of Mind

Understanding mean and trivial thoughts in the mind
One expels them with vigorous mindfulness.
An enlightened one has done with them all
For no more temptations then stir his mind.

THE BUDDHA

We have become infatuated with the surrounding world, and we use science and technology to make changes to it. Numerous sophisticated changes have occurred as a result of us using our minds and extending what previous generations have discovered or invented. There is much to be grateful for and much to be concerned about. As a conscious human being, we recognize the importance our part has to play in the scheme of things. We can all make a contribution to a sustainable world.

The Buddha encourages the development of real power of mind, without seeking ego gratification. If we experience and know these powers of mind, we feel stability and clarity within ourselves as well as a capacity to handle any external situation. The Buddha reminds us that we can develop each one of these powers of mind through the course of daily life. This supports right action and right action supports the power of mind.

Contact with like-minded people helps us receive support in terms of our growth as a human being and gives others support as well.

The two meditations included at the end of this chapter are *Meditation on the Sangha* and *Meditation on Nowhere to Go*.

Mindfulness not only includes concern about what we buy and the materials we use but also what happens to the packaging and waste, such as paper and cardboard, plastic and metal, bottles, and food.

It is worthwhile making an effort to ensure that waste products are recycled. Some European countries provide three or four waste bins to ensure that this happens, and many places have paper and bottle banks. All this represents a conscious awareness and the resolve to use such services.

In the old Buddhist texts, there is a reminder of the importance of making full use of what one has. The Buddha was asked what should be done with monk's robes when they had completely worn out. He advised that the cloth should be used for such things as cleaning the floor. He was then asked what should be done with the cloth when it's no longer useful for cleaning the floor. He advised that pieces of the cloth could be used for filling in holes and cracks in walls.

It means developing a caring attitude toward all things from beginning through to end, taking to heart the principle of "waste not, want not." This kind of approach will contribute to a sustainable world. For if we go on relentlessly producing, consuming, and blindly throwing away our surplus items onto the great rubbish heaps in and around our cities, we will almost certainly eventually create more and more problems for ourselves.

Working for the welfare of oneself, of others, and of the planet becomes an inspiration to take further steps, not only for quiet purposeful change but also to enlighten our life. We may need to speak with friends and family about making changes to develop and support a post-consumer society based on an enlightened attitude to living wisely. There are also a variety of organizations committed to such changes. It is from such small seeds that big trees grow.

RIGHT ACTION

If we consider right action, we see that it has an obvious relationship with taking a step back from self-interest, and from this vantage point we can see clearly the connection between action and result. There are primarily four kinds of action, and it might well be that we only concentrate on one or two of them at the expense of the others. The four kinds of action are:

❖ Action for the purpose of production, for example food, information, goods, and children
❖ Action for the purpose of reaching a destination whether by foot, bicycle, car, train, aeroplane etc
❖ Action for the purpose of modification, including everything from DIY in the home to modifying things to make them better
❖ Action for the purpose of development, including working on oneself (mind, heart, and spiritual life), and action for the welfare of others to give them support. We can work to develop the lives of people and animals as well as develop an enlightened attitude to the environment

Whether farmers use traditional methods or the latest machinery, it still requires hard work to produce food to feed the world's population.

When we look at ourselves, we need to take a long hard look at each of the four actions. Perhaps we recognize that exaggerated attention to only one or two occurs at the expense of the others. A common link that unites all four is the attitude and quality of our actions. These two factors matter as much as the results, though we tend to forget this. Clearness of mind functions as the focal point for these actions, but it is all too easy for our selfish desires to replace this. When this happens we think of development in a narrow and imbalanced way, and stop developing as a human being at both our personal cost and at the cost of the world we live in.

We tend to view the results of our actions as a comment on the condition of the self, but viewing them in this way only feeds our ego. We either boost ourselves up or put ourselves down. Our dependency on results makes us feel unsettled. Sometimes we wonder why our life seems so unsettled. It might be the consequence of past actions, but we might also be pursuing so many different ends that we have disregarded any real steadiness of mind in daily life. A boat that loses its rudder is in great danger of crashing on the reef.

FIVE MENTAL POWERS

If we are to approach action and results with skill, we need to develop a quality of mind that can deal skillfully with unfolding events. The Buddha listed five important areas to develop for skillful action, and referred to them as the Five Mental Powers:

❖ Trust—a sustained confidence in what we do through noble intention

❖ Mindfulness—the capacity to stay in touch with the process

❖ Meditative concentration—the ability to stay steady and clear in changing situations

❖ Energy—the willingness to arouse and sustain energy to bring tasks to completion

❖ Wisdom—to know what is skillful action and to be able to accommodate the results

All five powers of mind contribute significantly to supporting and strengthening our inner life, and enable us to work with issues, both inner and outer. If we are keenly interested in working on ourselves, then we can look at our relationship to each of these Five Mental Powers.

TRUST

There are often several times during the course of a day that we show a lack of confidence in what we say or do. This easily becomes a daily pattern that inhibits us from responding to situations in a clear and purposeful way. We get so used to this that we find ourselves showing a lack of confidence and trust, even talking about it with others as though we had no choice in the matter.

We need to make a firm resolution with ourselves that we will not give our doubts any authority over what we say or do. For example, if there is something that we wish to communicate to another, we may experience doubts in our mind and give lots of reasons to justify these doubts.

One person, a secretary, told me that she needed to speak frankly to her boss at work. He never seemed to have a kind word to say about anybody, whether working for the company or in his personal life. She thought of him as Whining Will. She kept her peace for months and months until she remembered the often-quoted statement of the Buddha, namely to speak what is both true and useful. It wasn't easy for her to speak up, so she prepared herself carefully. She recalled the incidents when he got lost in his cynical tirades as precisely as possible. One morning, before he began dictating the letters to her, she told him in a matter-of-fact way about her concerns. She said she did not want to be on the receiving end of his whining any longer. To his credit, he apologized. He said he hadn't realized how much he had got caught up in this pattern. The secretary was expressing the power of mind in her trust and confidence in her capacity to speak up.

Fear or hesitation that holds us back from speaking our thoughts reveals a lack of power to the mind. We have to make a quiet resolution to communicate what needs to be stated. There is of course some risk involved: we may get rejected, we may be misunderstood, or our words, no matter how skillfully expressed, may land on deaf ears. It is trusting in our perceptions that matters, even if the outcome is different from what we would wish.

At times, it is difficult to express trust in wholesome situations and ourselves. Trust reduces anxiety and despair as well as the less intense feelings of weakness and vulnerability. Everything happens in the present; even the highest mountain can only be climbed one step at a time. We may have to find ways and means to practice confidence in daily life, including communicating with people where we feel we can be heard. It may mean taking new initiatives that we would normally neglect, or even just learning to walk with a firm and confident stride so that we feel our inner authority.

It is these kinds of steps, both actual and metaphorical, that help in practical ways to cultivate the power of the mind so that we are able to respond to situations where normally we would find ourselves behaving passively. Trust and confidence also help us to be alone. We need confidence to be alone, to act independently even if we get disapproval from those who remain important to us. We can try starting our day reflecting on how to express trust during the day.

It is important that we sustain vigilance to guard against the ego building itself up on the back of confidence. The ego may show itself when we cling tightly to views and opinions, are unable to listen to others, and are arrogant, making others feel uncomfortable or oppressed. True confidence does not need the ego to boast about what we have done, are doing, or intend to do. The raw material for developing confidence emerges out of our relationship with day-to-day situations that challenge us to take steps when normally we would hesitate. Surely every day in some way or other gives us the opportunity to cultivate this power of mind.

Whether young or old, we sometimes need the loving support of another who understands the difficulty we are passing through.

MINDFULNESS

I have already referred to the great importance of mindfulness, which is the capacity to develop a moment-to-moment attention so that we feel connected with what is unfolding as it unfolds. The power of mindfulness contributes to an intimate connection with whatever we are engaged in at the time. When we lose the power of mindfulness, we easily subject ourselves to a whole range of projections, fantasies, and misperceptions.

The power of mindfulness enables us to cut through mental proliferation so that we abide in a calm and steady way, no matter what the task. We have the opportunity to practice mindfulness through all our circumstances. One famous and much loved Buddhist monk from Vietnam, Venerable Thich Nhat Hahn, wrote a piece about thirty years ago on the value of mindfulness while washing up. The following quotation has been pinned up in the kitchen of several Buddhist retreat centers around the world, and probably hundreds of homes. The essence of the quote reminds all of us that when we wash up we must be

PRACTICES FOR TODAY 1

1

Find an opportunity to extend trust

2

Make sure it is an action that is worthwhile

3

Stay with the action or commitment, without dependency on results

4

Remember to go a step further than the initial resistance

5

Remember trust dissolves the tendency to hold back and develops a power of mind mindful of that activity alone so that we do not put ourselves under pressure to simply get the task over and done with.

While washing the dishes, one should only be washing the dishes, which means that while washing the dishes one should be completely aware of the fact that one is washing the dishes. There are two ways to wash the dishes. The first is to wash the dishes in order to have clean dishes and the second is to wash the dishes in order to wash the dishes. If while washing dishes, we think only of the cup of tea that awaits us, thus hurrying to get the dishes out of the way as if they were a nuisance, then we are not washing the dishes to wash the dishes. If we can't wash the dishes, the chances are that we won't be able to drink our tea either.

We need to ensure we have time for sublime leisure so that we feel at ease with existence.

Mindfulness has to be accompanied with a genuine ethic so that it is not misused. For example, the burglar has a high degree of mindfulness as he goes from one room to the next searching for valuables during the night hours. He picks up every sound, he is aware of every single step that he takes and his fingers move gently through the drawers while the occupants of the house sleep on. This is certainly mindfulness without any ethical consideration.

When we are mindful of circumstances we incorporate a genuine interest in the intention that supports the mindfulness. The ego corrupts mindfulness through the desire to impress others with our mindfulness. On such occasions the quality of interest in the activity itself is lowered and the desire for attention and approval is heightened. Being mindful is a pure expression of connection with what is happening from one moment to the next. It is undiluted and untarnished by the demands of the self

so that mindfulness has the strength and quality to make it a power of the mind. The first power of the mind, trust, gives support to the second power of the mind, mindfulness.

MEDITATIVE CONCENTRATION

There is a growing public recognition that meditation has a vital part to play in enabling us to live a wise and sane life. We often forget that our mind is a limited resource, unable to withstand the relentless pressure on it through the desire for pleasure, experiences, and information. The mind needs to find rest and know inner contentment, and meditation makes a significant contribution. Not surprisingly, the Buddha made meditative concentration the eighth factor of the Noble Eightfold Path.

We are constantly telling ourselves and anyone else willing to listen that we need to slow down or stop, to have a break from a life of constant doing. Meditation is an important and valid interruption to constant activity. It provides us with a real opportunity to expose our whole being to a sublime stillness and sense of presence. If we are willing to create time in our daily life for meditation, we can renew contact with ourselves and simultaneously allow the mind to refocus, ground itself, and stay steady despite the pushes and pulls of different circumstances.

It is unwise to engage in consistent and uninterrupted use of our brain while we are awake because we will feel tired mentally, emotionally, and physically. Meditation develops concentration, and helps us keep a steadfastness of posture, relaxed breathing, a calm presence, and insight into states of mind and thought processes. It supports our life and cultivates a genuine power of mind. In meditation we are given the opportunity for our brain cells to become quiet and to discover a greater sense of harmony between body and mind. Through meditation, we find we can concentrate on necessary work instead of starting tasks and not finishing them,

or not even starting them at all. The power we develop from meditative concentration protects us from getting overwhelmed by tasks.

ENERGY

We are used to the scientific community, as well as economists and politicians, discussing energy resources, and their exploitation and use to meet demands of contemporary society. We also have to take equal note of our own energy reserves and how we use our energy in daily life. A growing number of people experience problems with their energy levels. Numerous factors from the past and the present have

It is worthwhile to find time for meditation for calmness and clarity about mental processes.

an impact on the quality of the energy that we have in daily life, but as energy capacity varies from one person to the next, there is little point in comparing ourselves with others.

It is helpful to look at the totality of each day in as practical a way as possible. We can usefully divide the day up into four periods:

❖ From waking to breakfast
❖ From breakfast to lunch
❖ From lunch to tea or dinner
❖ From tea or dinner to sleep

To get to know ourselves in terms of our energy flow is to give equal care and consideration to all four periods of the day. It is too easy to describe ourselves as a morning person or night person as a way of ignoring the other times of the day. We generate an imbalance in our day through an excessive output of energy during one period, and so we end up feeling utterly exhausted, restless, and unfocused during all the other periods.

WISDOM

The Buddhist tradition rightly emphasizes wisdom in all things, but in Western culture this has never had the central place it deserves. Instead, we have focused on identification with social and religious beliefs, and a spectrum of political, economic, and cultural objectives. All these influence society, giving shape and direction to our lives. Some of these features we appreciate and some we question.

However, it is a different matter with wisdom. Wisdom has at its core a relationship to daily life, creating an absence of suffering and dissatisfaction, together with the ability to see things clearly so that we do not generate problems for ourselves either in the present or in the future. Wisdom genuinely protects the mind and does not place burdens on others through our desires or through feeling needy. The power of wisdom not only allows us to see things clearly but also provides us with the capacity to respond to what we need, and to respond to and let

go of what we might react to. Wisdom plays a crucial role in mindful living.

We do not acquire wisdom in a sudden flash out of nowhere, though it can come as an intuitive insight. Rather, it is the outcome of the other four powers of mind. If we are willing to cultivate trust, mindfulness, meditation, and skillful use of our daily energy, we will discover wisdom.

In the Orient, sculptures indicate the importance of association with wise beings.

Wisdom and understanding mutually support each other and are in turn supported by trust and confidence. Sometimes we have more confidence than wisdom and we realize this when things start going wrong. Sometimes we confuse wisdom with knowledge; we then become very conceited, or increasingly philosophical.

Try to generate time to examine each of the Five Mental Powers, to see what might be useful to cultivate and practice in the course of daily life. We should not forget that these powers of mind act as a benevolent force. If we develop each power of mind, we will know that we can meet others on an equal level, and we will not feel intimidated by anybody else, nor feel the need to put them down.

The Five Mental Powers of mind all matter equally. Each one of them contributes significantly to enlightening our life and remaining receptive to a liberated dimension of being.

FINDING A TEACHER

Some people imagine what it would be like to have a spiritual teacher as their guide and shining light from one day to the next, and it is very rare for a person to rely upon themselves as the only source for finding wisdom. We may ask ourselves whether we need a teacher, and indeed it is the teachings that matter most—teachers simply serve as a vehicle for the teachings. This means that we can look at the value of teachers and our relationship with them in particular ways. It is certainly helpful to find a wise teacher. People may have one main teacher plus other teachers, or rely on several teachers equally.

In a relationship to a teacher, the student of Buddhism has the responsibility to distinguish the facts from the claims. It is not unusual for teachers to try to persuade their students to stay with them exclusively. They may claim that their teachings are in some way or other special, or say other

PRACTICES FOR TODAY 2

1

If you start a major action today,
be clear about the intention

2

See if the intention remains the same or changes
later in the day

3

Would you describe the intention as healthy,
unhealthy, or neutral?

4

Are there any kinds of actions to which you are overcommitted?

5

Are there any kind of actions that you neglect?
See what changes you can make

*We are on the move so much
in our daily life that we rarely
allow ourselves to stop and
reflect on our relationship to
life's deeper issues.*

teachers are not as good as they are. It is often difficult to prove or disprove the claims of teachers. For example, a teacher might belong to a long-standing tradition or lineage dating back thousands of years. On hearing this claim the student may have to consider the simple question: "This is what the teacher believes, but do I have to?"

Teachers sometimes make promises such as: "If you stay with me for a certain period of time, you will achieve a certain state." Such claims carry an arrogance and exploit a student's search for depth of experience. Teachers may claim all manner of enlightened states for themselves, but these are difficult to prove or disprove. It is important to remember that teachers are not perfect. They make mistakes and errors of judgment. The function of a tablecloth is not ruined because of a stain on it.

Regular contact with a spiritual teacher or teachers is an important aspect of spiritual development.

When choosing a teacher, find out the attitude and views of senior students associated with that teacher for a long time. Do they show wisdom and compassion? Do they reveal a depth of experience and insight? Are they imitating their teacher, through mannerisms, use of language, and other claims? A thoughtful student must not be afraid to weigh up these considerations in their own mind. We may stay with a teacher for any appropriate period of time, but we must also be ready to move on when it seems necessary. The first and only responsibility of a serious student is realizing an enlightened life, not staying loyal to a particular teacher. One expression of an enlightened life is freedom from attachment.

Initially, words such as God, enlightenment, truth, and reality may seem like vague concepts to the dedicated seeker. These concepts can become even more confusing when so many different faces of authority have different definitions of these words. Any teacher can become attached to their own explanation and dismiss the definition of others, but

such a teacher has forgotten that words, like everything else, have no inherent meaning. Words are defined by their use.

It is a hopeless task trying to discover a common view and perception among spiritual teachers, and the spiritual tradition shows as much diversity and inconsistency as anything else when it comes to finding agreement about what matters and what words mean. It is a bit of a minefield in the spiritual world, where priorities, behavior, and values seem often to be in conflict with each other. But, despite the incongruousness of this, it is worth continuing in order to get through to the other side. Morality (non-harming), meditation, and wisdom are what matter.

TRANSCENDENCE

The variety of words used to communicate the ultimate truth of things can seem baffling. We might feel that achieving enlightenment is nearly impossible, and ordinariness of our own lives makes enlightenment seem countless lifetimes away. This encourages us to

Be aware of the powers of your mind, and make the most of them during quiet moments in the day.

think that enlightenment is a special state, only achieved by very rare human beings. We then draw the conclusion that at best we can only make a few tentative steps toward such an exalted state.

Diligent practice, experience of meditation, and skillful teachings can dig deep into such a cherished view. What were faraway and seemingly unreachable ideals suddenly become much closer. The dedicated practitioner can know what it means to be on the edge of enlightenment, to feel very close to utter awakening in the here and now. It has been said before and it is worth saying again that before enlightenment, it seems mysterious and faraway, but after enlightenment it becomes part of the ordinary and everyday. This brings a complete reversal; much of the conditioned mind, with its views and reactive attitudes, seems far away and mercifully unobtainable.

Meditation on the Sangha

The word sangha literally means "gathering." It refers to two or more people gathered together to explore the Dharma, the teachings and practices that enlighten our life. The Buddha, Dharma, and Sangha have more value than possession of all the jewels placed together of all the royal families in the world. The Buddha-Dharma-Sangha reveal three expressions of the greatest jewel available to humanity. Like a precious diamond, this jewel exists in the world to point the way to the utter resolution of suffering at every level.

I regard the sangha as supportive friends
I place my trust and confidence in the sangha
I regard the sangha as worthy of deepest respect
I take my inspiration from the sangha so that I can let
  go of what I need to let go of
Renounce what I need to renounce
Develop what I need to develop
And overcome what I need to overcome
Through my commitment to the sangha
I pay respect to the sangha
Without the sangha, I fall back on my self with its
  unwise and unskillful tendencies
With the support of the sangha, I can see clearly so that
  I fall back on wisdom within and truly act as a noble
  one
I know that my teachers belong to the sangha support
  the sangha and nourish the sangha and that my
  teachers and seniors in the sangha welcome the
  wisdom of the sangha so that they remain true to a
  noble way of life
The sangha is worthy of attention, worthy of merit
  worthy of support, worthy of commitment
May I be willing to give support to the sangha as an
  expression of dana* whether it is through time,
  energy, work, practice, offerings, sums of money and
  frequent presence so that the sangha abides in unity,
  in love, and in harmony always remaining respectful
  to the Noble Ones to Liberation and to an
  Enlightened Life

*donations, gifts, offerings, acts of generosity

Meditation on Nowhere to Go

Establish a firm, upright posture. Keep the posture very still for five minutes. With the back straight, settle into the moment.

There is nothing that I want
There is nothing to run after
I have nothing to do
I have nowhere to go
I cannot add to what is present already
I cannot take away from what is present already
Sights come to my eyes
Sounds come to my ears
Smells come to my nose
Tastes come to my tongue
Touch comes to my body
Thoughts and feelings come to my mind
I cannot add to these experiences
I cannot subtract from them
It has been like this as long as I can remember
I abide calmly knowing this
I abide in this simple truth
Knowing that there is nothing more to be done

Buddhist monks have a deep love of the forest. Trees remind us of their important place on earth and the value of an upright life.

Mindfulness of Right Speech

Practice lovingkindness to get rid of ill will
Practice compassion to get rid of cruelty
Practice appreciative joy to get rid of apathy
Practice equanimity to get rid of resentment

THE BUDDHA

Right speech, one of the factors of the Noble Eightfold Path, says as much about ourselves as it does about what we talk about. The Buddha advised that we remember to speak what is true and useful. Sometimes people get the idea that Buddhism and meditation are one and the same thing. If we give care and consideration to what we say, we will deserve the trust of people that we have contact with.

Others will treat our words with caution, if we lie, exaggerate, or gossip. Gossip and rumors generate anguish and problems when perceptions of situations become distorted. The teachings of the Buddha consider it an action of compassion not to spread gossip.

If we give our words, spoken or written, the highest priority then we will find many other areas of our life will fall into a proper perspective. We sometimes exaggerate our own situation, for better or worse, and that has its own consequences. There is integrity in developing right speech. It also contributes to peace of mind.

The two meditations for this chapter are *Meditation on Compassion* and *Meditation on Absence of.*

Right speech makes a real difference to the quality of our lives. The most important words, spoken or written, then become insights that enable us to overcome greed, hate, and delusion (known in the Buddhist tradition as the three poisons of the mind). Important words open the heart, calm the mind, and help us realize an enlightened life. If we give these words the highest priority, then all other words will be put into perspective.

In everyday communication, there is a flow from the inner to the outer. The basis for communication begins with our perceptions and feelings about a person, place, idea, or whatever we are referring to. The perceptions and feelings become thoughts, then those thoughts become actualized as the spoken word or written words. We want what we say or write to make an impact, or at least leave an impression upon others. We also need to choose carefully what we listen to or read so that it leaves a worthwhile impression upon us. The word becomes flesh.

Words never exist totally by themselves but only in relationship to the mind that is expressing or receiving them. Neither does any word possess any inherent self-existent meaning. Two people can interpret the same word, phrase, or theme in similar or dissimilar ways. At times, it may be necessary to reflect back to the other person what we have heard, to check that we have understood what they have said or that they have understood what we have said.

THREE IMPORTANT CONSIDERATIONS

Three important considerations contribute to making our speech as effective as possible. They are:

> ❖ Intentions
> ❖ Attitudes
> ❖ Tone of voice

Practice in communication means learning to speak with an intention not to cause harm. We endeavor to express an attitude that shows a wholesome as well as a balanced view of a situation. We speak or write in a tone of voice that shows a caring and thoughtful concern for the circumstances.

The Buddha said that true speech is "distinct, intelligent, deep, and decisive." It is not unusual for us to express our views and opinions on matters about

Laughter and playfulness belong to the passion of life. A warm heart informs the words we use.

which we know little except what we have heard, seen on television, or read in the newspapers. Sometimes it would be useful to admit our ignorance about certain matters, and observe a noble silence rather than throw out opinions that are based on an incomplete understanding of a situation.

What we know, we express to others. It may be true and useful, or unskillful to the point that our words feed prejudices, within and without. For the word to become flesh, it must show a depth of clarity, honesty, and wisdom.

We often find ourselves speaking at much the same level of conversation day in and day out. Our conversations easily become restricted to talking of the past, the present, the future, and various matters of self-interest. What we talk about reveals our values, priorities, and general sense of purpose in life. To some degree, we are known for what we say. We may not think so, but it is mostly how other people know us.

We need to develop a genuinely deep wish to probe more thoroughly into this matter of wise speech. However, any attempts to probe deeper seem difficult due to the discomfort that others experience when profound questions are raised about what really matters. To even raise questions about the meaning of life can generate a stony silence in some people, and many people have no idea what it means to have a deep conversation.

ASKING THE RIGHT QUESTIONS

If we wish to direct a conversation to a deeper level, then several aspects or questions begin to arise. For example, a close friend comes to visit you, who obviously has a lot on her mind. She pours out a story about a major row she has had at home. She feels very upset and angry, and it is clear that she simply wants somebody to listen to her side of the story. As the listener, you may have to adopt a more neutral position rather than identify with her version of events. You can ask the following questions to help her get clear in herself:

❖ Do you want me to simply listen?
❖ What was your motivation or intention in the row?
❖ What can you learn from these circumstances?
❖ What do you need to change, let go, or remember?
❖ If you had the opportunity, how would you approach the situation differently?
❖ What do you need to be clear about in future?
❖ Is there anything that I can do to help resolve the conflict?

The world of communication often gives people a real headache, either before something is said, while it is said, or afterward—as a result of what the other person said or from the words that came out of our own mouth.

Once, when the Buddha stayed at Campa on the banks of the Gaggara Lake, householders and wanderers got into a discussion about the Buddha's teachings. The householder, Vajjhiyamahita, explained to the others that the Buddha spoke "with discrimination, not one who makes one-sided utterances." He said the Buddha only described "how certain things are wholesome and how certain things are unwholesome" rather than "condemning and censuring without qualification."

How many times in life have we said to ourselves, "Why did I say that? I should have kept my big mouth shut. It's only made matters worse." We forget that pressure easily builds up within us through our various perceptions, feelings, and thoughts. Unable to take the pressure, we get upset, not realizing how much tension we have accumulated. Before we know it, we express our views and opinions in an agitated and hostile manner.

The Value of Communication

Her husband tended to keep things to himself. He had a small company that he took care of, and had put many years of hard work into it just to stay afloat. He could not bear the thought of letting his family down or sacking his faithful employees. One morning at breakfast, his wife asked him directly about the financial state of the firm. He said he expected things to improve soon. She leaned on him harder, and it turned out that the whole future of his company rested on another company in deep financial trouble settling their account.

His wife hit the roof, and her husband then began to engage in heavy self-criticism, calling himself a failure. They found themselves in deep distress. Her anger had collided with his denial of reality in terms of the uncertain future of the company. She stayed at home feeling guilty about her overreaction while he drove off to work feeling that he could never do anything right. Anger never solves problems. It is like throwing water on a frying pan of burning cooking oil when the pan will only flare up in flames. We have to be very clear about communication and practice to soften our tone, soften our language, not raise our voice, and try to understand somebody rather than make their life more difficult than it already is.

Once, in a grove, the Buddha spotted some boys ill-treating fish. He went up to the boys and said: "Are you afraid of pain? Do you dislike pain? Who does not want to suffer should not do harmful deeds, openly or in secret. For later, though you may try to flee it, you surely will suffer."

RESPONSES TO QUESTIONS

To know ourselves well requires the ability to track ourselves from perceptions to feelings to right thought to speech and to the impact of what we say on others.

Sometimes someone may have a question that they wish to ask that only requires a simple answer. Unfortunately, our latent tendencies can have more influence on the way we answer than the content of the question itself. The Buddha reminds us that there are only four *verbal* responses—as well as silence—to respond to direct questions. These are:

❖ Yes
❖ No
❖ Both yes and no
❖ Don't know
❖ Observe noble silence

Any of these five responses may be necessary in a given situation. There is a famous example recorded in the New Testament. Pontius Pilate, the Roman governor of Palestine, asked Jesus before he was summarily tortured, "What is the truth?" Jesus observes noble silence rather than respond to an ignorant and arrogant man who has no real intention of listening to the truth of the teachings of Jesus.

There may be only a few occasions in our own life when it is necessary to observe noble silence in the face of questioning. There is also the legal allowance to keep silent in the courts of law. We must regard it as an important option.

Some of us have a strong desire to please others through seeking their approval. We may not agree with what they say, but we go along with their version of events. Consequently, we fail to express the truth as we see it. If we notice that we are falling into this trap, we must ask ourselves:

❖ Are we afraid of that person?
❖ Do we fear rejection?
❖ Do we want to be liked?
❖ Do we deny our perception and think they must know better than we do?

Some of us find it hard to keep a secret. We are told something in confidence, and make strong promises never to reveal a word of what we have been told to another. Within 24 hours, we have told others, asking them to keep it a secret. Sometimes it seems the best way to get

PRACTICES FOR TODAY 1

1
Go through today without talking behind another person's back

2
When you speak start off by saying "I believe... " rather than speaking with absolute certainty

3
Make your tone of speech softer, if it tends to be hard

4
Put questions to the person you are speaking to, rather than getting into a disagreement

5
Speak less hurriedly

A deep friendship with another develops through the capacity of two people to help each other.

information passed from one person to another is speaking in a confidential way! This gives the information a special flavor, which helps ensure that it travels quickly.

The inability of certain people to keep information confidential can be very distressing. Many close relationships go through a crisis period or break up because one person betrayed the other's trust by failing to protect some important information.

SAFEGUARDS IN SPEECH

There are several helpful safeguards that enable us to keep steady in our communication. We should be mindful of:

❖ What we say when speaking about a third person: would we use the same words and tone to their face?

❖ How much time do we spend engaged in superficial chatter: it is not unusual for superficial chatter to begin most conversations, but it takes skill and practice to take a superficial matter to a deeper exploration.

❖ What signals do we pick up from the person(s) listening to our words: some people have great difficulty in stopping talking once they have started, going on and on, unaware that their audience feels bored. Bored listeners generally put out clear signals that they are looking for a way out of the conversation.

A friend of mine met with a member of the British Royal family, who asked him one or two questions about his work. He said the member of the Royal Family looked at him with eyes wide open and said at the appropriate times, "yes… yes… yes…" But my friend got the impression that the member of the royal household had no real interest in what he had to say, and that he simply *appeared* interested. It was a pity that my friend did not ask the member of the Royal Family whether or not he was deliberately putting out a mixed message; it would have been interesting to hear the response.

Children share secrets. If adults are told something in confidence, we must keep it to ourselves.

Sometimes, there are clearly important things we wish to communicate, but it may take us some time to say what we want. We may feel the listener is attending to everything that we say, but as we finish talking, the other person may respond with "but …" They then begin to speak for the same amount of time that we had spoken for, if not longer. It leaves us with the impression that they were not really listening to us at all in the first place, but had simply waited for us to finish what we had to say so that the opposite viewpoint could be expressed. At times like this, communication can easily go down that slippery slope into an argument.

When two people hold contradictory views, often the two mind states cannot meet each other nor understand where the other is coming from. There is only one thing that can be said with some certainty: both people share the common view of feeling that they are right. So we must practice right speech and right listening daily to develop deep friendships, dissolve tension, overcome misunderstanding, and avoid entering into painful conflicts. Yet we must not be afraid to exchange strong differences of view on important matters.

Much interpersonal suffering arises through a lack of willingness to look at feelings, thoughts, speech, and the consequences of what is said. We often hear of politicians who make a public speech referring to matters of public concern. The politician knows that they have to tread very carefully, since the press will fasten onto one or two words or phrases to highlight or comment on in the following morning's newspapers. In such situations, it is very easy to take what is said out of context and build up a false picture of who the speaker is and what he or she stands for.

TREADING CAREFULLY

We are prone to doing the same thing ourselves, listening to what someone has said and selecting two or three things to remember. What we select may be telling us more about ourselves than about what the other person has said. We must tread carefully with what we say to avoid feeding conflicts between people through unwise recollection of what has been said.

The Buddhist tradition emphasizes repeatedly the great importance of wise speech. The greatest distortion of language occurs through intentionally telling a lie so that it brings harm and suffering to others, or is used to manipulate the mind of another to secure the maximum benefit or profit for oneself or another. We practice to keep steady with the truth, to spell it out sensitively and accurately and not become overwhelmed by pressure from within or without to distort the truth.

Some of the motivations for wilfully distorting our speech include:

❖ Desire to please
❖ Fear of being misunderstood
❖ Not wanting to take blame
❖ Dread of consequences
❖ Trying to create a certain impression

When we witness the embrace of two lovers, we might appreciate their happiness or we might feel jealous.

It isn't easy to find the courage to communicate what is both true and useful. The Buddha emphasized strongly that we should pay attention to speaking what is true and useful. He said that this is the criterion for meaningful conversation. The more we distort our words the less we are trusted. People create a distance from us because they cannot rely upon our honesty. Right speech means paying attention to the words we use and the way we use them as an indispensable feature of right living. The Buddha said that an awakened one understands "with its possibilities and reasons, the past, future, and present and the liability of actions to ripen." What we say can have a significant impact on our lives and the lives of others.

THE ART OF LISTENING

Over the last quarter of a century, I have facilitated thousands of groups, sometimes a number of groups in a single day. I have noticed again and again that in a group of eight or ten people, some want to speak more, some less, and some may have little or nothing to contribute, or they may *feel* they have very little to contribute to the discussion.

I have often noticed that asking a quiet person to add to the discussion has been eye-opening. People who are quiet often have much wisdom to share, but tend to hold back rather than be forthcoming. The facilitator may need to encourage the quiet ones to speak.

When it comes to speaking, we need to consider two features. We carry greater authority when we speak directly from our personal experience rather than thinking along purely theoretical lines. First-hand experience tends to arouse much more interest.

In speaking to others, we try to remain mindful that we do not fall into the trap of absolutism. The absolutist refuses to allow any other way of looking at a situation. Too many people adopt a point of view that there is only one true way to look at something, and they know what it is. It makes people hesitant, fearful, or upset when people feel they are being spoken at or spoken down to, and they regard it as a lack of respect to their experience and understanding.

It is important in such circumstances to speak provisionally. "It seems to me at the present time…," or "My experience tells me…," or "Currently, I have come to understand…," or "I believe that…" In any communication with a friend, or with a large audience, it requires a skillfulness to make sure we can be heard as clearly and as easily as possible. After all, we talk so that others will listen with interest to what we have to say. People cannot listen if we do not know how to talk respectfully to them. Wise speech is a genuinely daily practice that makes every communication a significant event. It is important that we remain vigilant about how much we use "I" and "my" and how willingly we listen to others.

If we engage in a discussion where participants hold significantly different

T'ai chi calms the mind and settles the body, enabling you to remain steady within.

When two people cook together neither should cling to an idea of how something should be done.

points of view, it takes calm awareness to know when to call an end to the communication. Anybody who holds to a position, identifies with it strongly and clings to it will block out other ways of looking at the issue. There are always contradictions in the inflexible mind. It takes skillful questioning to make a point using the contradiction, and then managing to end the conversation with an invitation for the other person to look at the contradiction. Otherwise, we can find ourselves battling with each other in a hopeless endeavor to score points through clinging to our position. There is no point whatsoever in taking responsibility for somebody else's inner world. We may be wise, skillful, insightful, and a master in communication, but that does not mean to say that we will make any impact on another's view if they have only one determination in their mind and that is to cling to their views no matter how harmful.

Most of us would probably agree that the sky appears blue, water is wet, and forests contain lots of trees. When someone claims that the sky does not appear blue, water is not wet, and there are no trees in a forest, there is not much that a Buddha can do about it. So it means that we have to be cognitive of situations and in some cases exercise much patience. Not surprisingly, the Buddhist tradition has wisely acknowledged the value of *skillful means*, a key concept in the Buddhist tradition concerned with dealing with problem situations.

SKILLFUL REFLECTION

There are two considerations in terms of skillful reflection before entering into a difficult communication with another:

❖ Does the subject merit such a communication?
❖ Is there the potential for harm or suffering?

A woman told me that her partner at home took his turn to cook the evening meal. She watched him prepare the food, but felt he lacked the culinary skills to prepare the sauce for the food correctly. She found herself becoming more irritated, and then tried to take over the task. He reacted and told her to cook the "whole damn meal" herself.

I told her that it sounded to me that she was clinging to her method and technique of cooking. She may not approve of his method of cooking but he would not cause any harm, while she was in danger of poisoning the relationship. We often think we know best in matters that really don't matter one iota.

In cases of potential suffering, the response is different, and we need to express our concern and to act skillfully. A two-year-old boy decided he wanted to help his mother cut up vegetables in the kitchen. He picked up the knife rather haphazardly and began cutting a carrot in rough pieces. His mother spotted

that he had the potential to cut himself. When she took the knife away from him, he started yelling and stamping his feet. The mother wisely interfered to safeguard her son from causing himself harm. Before we enter into a conversation with another person, we need to reflect on both the necessity and the potential benefits of it.

WISE ATTENTION

We have to develop the capacity to employ skillful means when a communication with another has gone badly wrong. There is no point in blaming the other person, nor ourselves, for the conflict and confusion that arises. Instead, we track back to the source of our attitudes that formed our contribution to a highly charged communication. If we go on ignoring the source of our reactivity, we will live trapped in the ego's determination to justify or condemn itself. We then turn our back on what matters, namely finding inner peace despite difficulties.

Wisdom reveals contentment with our own company whether we are young or old.

It is not enough to track back only as far as feelings and intentions, but it is creditable that you have reached back that far, especially if you remain truthfully connected with the depth of your inner life. Authentic steps in daily life need to take us backward as well as forward—backward to the causes and conditions for reactivity. Then we must accept the facts and learn from them.

WORDS AND THE BODY

Communication matters a great deal. It is no easy task to cross the bridge from language to experience and from experience to understanding. The most significant form of communication contributes directly to insight and realization rather than simply accumulating opinions and cerebral knowledge. We have to have understanding ourselves, if we hope to convey clarity to others.

For example, if we talk about love, compassion, and the welfare of others, we must apply these concerns to our daily life. We may not be *arahants* (fully realized) or *bodhisattvas* (utterly dedicated to compassionate action) but at least we can make a contribution to an enlightened life through serving others. It is easy to say what should be done and yet do next to nothing about it ourselves.

It is worthwhile making the effort to listen to people with experience and wisdom. It is a beautiful thing to be touched deeply as a result of listening to another person. Sometimes a few profound words can make a lasting impact on our life.

I remember when I was a Buddhist monk I received a letter from my mother expressing concern about some material thing that she cherished and had lost. In my reply to her, I said that nothing is worth clinging to. It is one of those simple truths that anybody who has any connection with the Buddhist tradition hears often enough. My mother wrote back to me and told me that those few words in my letter really made a difference to her. She gave up all of her concern about this lost item, together with the sentimental value it held. Years later, she told me she always remembers the importance of nonclinging whenever she has lost something.

PRACTICES FOR TODAY 2

1

Write a letter showing absence of malice

2

Try to be kind and factual

3

Read it through slowly and carefully again

4

Post the letter the day after writing it

5

Would you appreciate such a letter?

Words are important. If we write a serious letter, we might consider posting it a day later so that we can re-read the letter after a night's sleep.

DEEP LISTENING

There are times when we seem to have an unusual degree of receptivity that enables us to hear important reflections on life, and benefit from what we listen to. The insights may stay with us for many years. There is a world of difference between hearing something that just passes over our head and something that touches a deep place within. The Buddhist tradition emphasizes that meditation makes an important contribution to insight through listening. For example, it is not unusual in a meditation retreat for Dharma students to feel that the teacher gives the evening teachings directly for their own personal benefit.

Revealed insight shows the receptivity of the student as well as the skillfulness of the teacher. There is a potential through communication that can truly transform lives, and it is this form of communication that puts words to their best use. They are a great resource, and if they come out of deep experience, they have more power to them, whether we are speaking or listening.

Compassion expresses itself as an activity that helps relieve suffering. It makes life a noble undertaking.

In 1977, I recall visiting the University of California, Berkeley. I had arrived in San Francisco after about ten years in the East, including six years as a Buddhist monk. A friend, studying Buddhism at the university, invited me to come to listen to the class. Naturally enough, I was interested and sat quietly and inconspicuously at the back of the class.

The lecturer spoke about the differences between the arahant and the bodhisattva in Buddhism. However, right at the end of the lecture, the professor got very angry when he spotted me sitting at the back of the lecture room. Banging his fist on his desk, he demanded to know why a stranger was attending his lectures without prior permission. All the students turned their heads to look around to see who he was referring to. I smiled, apologized, and got up to leave the room. I smiled because the lecturer had spent the last 45 minutes talking about saving all sentient beings, relieving suffering, and the benefits of following the path of the bodhisattva. Judging from the lecturer's reaction, the word was not made flesh.

Let us practice so that we experience harmony between speech and action as much as possible. It is an enormous challenge.

Meditation on Compassion

I do not have to look very far to see suffering in this
world

I know that pity is not the same as compassion

Compassion calls me to respond, to offer words, gestures,
gifts

Compassion demands something from my love, from
concern

I cannot ignore what I know

I can only respond as best I can

I am not perfect

I am not a Buddha or a Christ
yet, I can respond

I can offer something

I can share something

I can express something that reveals a compassionate
concern

I know that my gestures for others are as nothing
compared to the suffering in the world yet, I act
anyway

Never expecting anything in return

Knowing that it is a small token

But these gestures of love, regularly expressed reveal
my humanity

Take the power out of selfishness

In addition, they show that we are all connected in
this web of life together

Meditation on Absence of

Sometimes we get stuck with views about ourselves
that are untrue and unfair, and as a result we see
ourselves in the worst possible light. Others also do
that when they make harsh generalizations about us.
This meditation makes clear to us the lack of inherent
truth in the tendency to put others or ourselves
down. We become much more mindful of bare
actuality. We practice these meditations when there is
nothing in particular going on in our mind.

Right now, I experience the absence of any anger

Right now, I am not caught up in the judgmental mind

Right now, I am not blaming myself

Right now, I am not blaming anyone else

Right now, I know the impermanence of my negative
views

Right now, I know the impermanence of the harsh critic
within myself

Right now, I know how false it is to say "always,"
"never," "only"

I am mindful of the absence of unpleasant states
of mind

I am mindful of not being in conflict with others
or myself

I am mindful of the absence of intense thoughts
and ideas

I am mindful of feeling cool inside and not burning up

I am mindful of the absence of fixations about anything

I am mindful of the absence of trying to use my
will-power

I am mindful that this troublesome mind state came and
went like a dream

Mindfulness of Five Precepts and Seven Ways for Inner Change

What is the jewel of wisdom?
It is through wisdom that one comprehends
what is unwholesome and wholesome,
what is blameworthy and blameless,
what is low and excellent,
what is suffering and the way leading to end it.

THE BUDDHA

The main body of the Buddha's teachings covers three primary areas: ethics, meditation, and wisdom. In that respect there is nothing particularly religious or philosophical about his teachings, since he formulated them as a practice for our deepest well-being. We have to see through our own experience the value of the teachings, rather than simply agree or disagree with them.

Much of what the Buddha says makes simple common sense. It is not likely that we shall read or hear anything in his teachings that we do not know already. The key that runs through the body of teachings is practice, practice, practice, until we understand the joy and delight of penetrating the reality of things.

The Buddha was once asked: "Why do we develop the Noble Eightfold Path and cultivate ethics, meditation, and wisdom?" He replied very simply: "Because it is the happiest way to live." The practice opens up our hearts to a different way of seeing things, while the here and now becomes the open doorway to a liberated life.

Two meditations in this chapter are *Meditation on Love* and *Meditation on Liberation*.

PRACTICES FOR TODAY 1

1

Try to overcome a single resistance that blocks
a skillful activity

2

Breathe in and out through wavering thoughts

3

Take steps from the known to the unknown

4

Make use of your right effort and determination

5

If one resistance is too hard,
make sure you break through another

*A Buddhist monk climbs the steps of
a temple. This reminds us of the
steps we need to find what is sacred.*

There are millions of people in the East who look to Buddhism for an appropriate view of reality. If you take a cursory look at the religion, you might think that it is mostly about rebirth and that we will all move on to a better life if we do good by making merit in this life. This view is very common, and has certainly become more popular during the past 2,500 years. For the wise, views about the future exist only as views about the future.

Buddhist teachings strongly emphasize the importance of experience. What this means is that we cannot confirm directly rebirth through experience; that it happens only can be inferred. There is no direct proof of it. It is similar to believing in heaven or hell:

The Buddha gave his first teachings in the Deer Park in Sarnath, India. He spoke about the middle way.

we can believe, disbelieve, or be unsure. We may consider that life keeps engaging in a process of beginning, ending, and beginning again in ever-changing ways, but we cannot say for certain that there is rebirth or not.

Once a man was trying to find fault with the Buddha. He wanted to put him down by criticizing his teaching so he sent his son to talk with the Buddha. The father said to the son, "Go and find out what he is teaching." The son went to the Buddha and asked him. The Buddha replied, "I teach virtue." "What is virtue?" inquired the son, and the Buddha said, "It is not causing suffering through body, speech, and mind."

The son went back to his father and told him, "He is teaching virtue." His father said, "Well, I can't find anything wrong with that. Go back and see if he is teaching anything else."

The son went back to the Buddha and asked, "Are you teaching anything else?" The Buddha replied, "Yes, I'm teaching meditative concentration." He added, "Meditative concentration brings oneness of mind." In other words, if the mind is very scattered, it means it lacks samadhi. A scattered mind sees things as alluring and enticing, attractive or repulsive.

The son went back and told his father. His father said, "Go back and see if he is teaching anything else."

The son went back to the Buddha. He asked, "Sir, are you teaching anything else?" The Buddha said, "Yes, I'm teaching wisdom." "What is wisdom?" asked the son. The Buddha replied, "Wisdom comes through developing virtue and samadhi. Wisdom understands the conditioned phenomena of things, how they arise and pass. This is wisdom."

So the son went back and reported this to his father. His father said, "Go back and see if he is teaching anything else."

The son went back to the Buddha and asked, "Are you teaching anything else?" The Buddha replied, "No, I only teach virtue, meditative concentration,

A Tibetan monk says goodbye before going on pilgrimage to the holy places in India.

and wisdom." The father could not find fault and embraced the teaching.

FIVE PRECEPTS

The Buddhist tradition says that virtue is based on the five precepts, but these are not regarded as commandments in the way that we would understand in the Jewish and Christian tradition. They are aspects of a training to live life wisely. The five precepts are:

❖ I undertake the training not to engage in killing

❖ I undertake the training not to engage in stealing

❖ I undertake the training not to engage in sexual abuse

❖ I undertake the training not to engage in lying

❖ I undertake the training not to abuse alcohol and drugs

It is clear that the mode of instruction is in the form of the *absence* of. Our life is of a different order when we commit ourselves with a wholehearted endeavor to observe and be respectful to each of these five precepts. It is worthwhile exploring in more detail the five precepts so that we develop them in a subtle way. We then practice to undertake a training to give support to life in all of its forms.

FIRST PRECEPT   I will help to protect life rather than destroy it. I will support those voices that seek for reconciliation, harmony, and justice for one and all. I make a commitment to protecting life rather than justifying war, executions, and experiments on animals. I will give as much support as I can to the welfare of people, animals, and other sentient beings, recognizing their right to life. I will treat with respect creatures that live on the ground, in the water, and in the air. I will endeavor to support their habitat. I acknowledge the importance of biodiversity in the world. I regard the first precept as a training for the mind in developing expressions of lovingkindness for all beings, great and small.

SECOND PRECEPT   I undertake the training to share and give rather than take. Instead of regarding things as mine or as belonging to myself, I will treat things in a different way. I will try not to take too much from life itself so that others can have the opportunity to feel better off. I will develop a generous heart that is expansive and supportive. If I know that something does not belong to me, I will leave it alone or hand it in to the appropriate authority. I will endeavor to check with another that whatever I use I have permission to use from the appropriate person. I undertake the practice to remain mindful of other people's possessions. I will bring mindfulness to whatever I have contact with, treating money, goods, and items with care and respect to make them last.

When we experience the painful consequences of actions we may seek the loving support of another.

THIRD PRECEPT   I undertake the training to be sensitive and respectful in matters of sexuality, rather than engage in the manipulation of another person or persons. I will be aware of how powerful sexual energy is. I will take care with its expression so that any sexual activity is supported with kindness, love, and warmth. I will make this my commitment so that I do not confuse short-term pleasure with deep connection and communication. I will ensure that sexual life and genuine love do have a relationship together. I will practice to ensure that my sexual

energies do not become separated from matters of the heart. I will remain respectful to people's gender preferences between consenting adults rather than develop prejudices in such matters. I will take care with health and pregnancy issues out of concern for others and myself. I will remain respectful to my roles and privileges and will not use them for my own personal advantage.

FOURTH PRECEPT   I will bring awareness to speech so that what I say is accurate and beneficial. I will use speech that is appropriate and thoughtful, mirroring the reality of circumstances as much as possible. If at times I need to speak with firmness, I will do so in a spirit of expressing deep concern rather than in an arrogant or judgmental manner. Realizing how gossip, backbiting, and irresponsible talk causes difficulty, if not suffering, I will endeavor to make right speech a central feature of my inner development. I will practice not to raise my voice in a disagreement nor try to force my views upon another. I will practice to keep my body language calm and

steady so that neither my words, nor my physical presence appear to impose a threat to another. When I will disagree with another I will not make the disagreement a means to fuel anger and hatred. I will find the courage to speak up to help stop suffering.

FIFTH PRECEPT   I will practice to keep my mind calm and clear and refuse any substances that affect my state of mind. I will practice to develop close connections with nature and experience the natural highs of such experiences, rather than use intoxicants to induce artificially changes in consciousness. I will keep my senses and heart open as much as possible to all that life offers without trying to escape from circumstances through alcohol or drugs. I will trust in the process of things and the value of practicing to stay steady from one day to the next. By staying away from exposure to alcohol and drugs, and addictive substances like nicotine, I give further protection to

If we lie or distort the truth, we can end up in endless arguments trying to justify ourselves.

A healthy relationship means that two people face the same direction in terms of awareness and love.

my physical life in the short and long term. If I drink alcohol, it is in moderation. It is simply for enjoying the taste and not for use as a mood-changing substance. I will avoid the use of any illegal drugs for recreational or spiritual purposes since they contribute to supporting addictive personalities; unwise company; secret, illegal laboratories; and drug barons.

SEVEN WAYS FOR INNER CHANGE

The Buddhist tradition has pointed how important it is to see into our personal problems so that we can take the power out of them, leaving our mind clear and content. There is much emphasis on meditation and mindfulness to give support to moving from one situation to the next. The Buddha has reflected on various ways that we need to consider to overcome personal difficulties. We have to give attention to

different methods and sustain them until personal suffering is resolved. No one is saying that it is easy. It is important, however, that we take a broad approach to finding peace of mind rather than thinking that mindfulness answers everything. It is easy to think that seeing a problem gives us enough power to dissolve the problem. This is not always the case.

We can easily invest too much in developing mindfulness and meditation as a kind of medicine to cure the entire range of inner difficulties. We can find ourselves taking up this position rather than recognizing such practices as making an important contribution to ethics, meditative concentration, and wisdom. In one of his talks, the Buddha listed seven considerations for inner change. We may need to develop one or more of them until we have established wisdom around that particular issue.

The seven considerations are:

- Seeing
- Restraining
- Making use of
- Enduring
- Avoiding
- Removing
- Developing

SEEING I believe it is true to say that there is a remarkable power to meditation. It has an extraordinary capacity to develop the mind to stay present, focused, and concentrated on the immediate. People who meditate on a regular basis report the benefits that it brings to their inner life. Some say that it makes them more productive and creative in their particular field due to the mental energy that meditation can release. These benefits cannot be overlooked, but our capacity to see and act needs the support of inner change through ethical foundations, concern for others, and concern for the environment. Seeing clearly matters. From seeing, we devote ourselves to staying awake, keeping the heart open, and tasting the sweetness of freedom.

It is important also that we do not deceive ourselves. If we see clearly, it truly makes a difference; if we do not see clearly, then it does not. If we see clearly, we will act directly or make use of one or more of the other six considerations for overcoming problems. We may talk about our problems with others, or think about them, but we do have to be clear within ourselves that our primary intention is to resolve them. This is a very important point. It is often necessary to keep checking with ourselves on a daily basis that we truly have every intention to resolve a problem as quickly as possible. If that is the case, then following the seven considerations will make a genuine difference.

The seven considerations should run together within your mind, becoming a coherent whole.

Seeing truly helps to break and dissolve those unsatisfactory states of mind that arise in the present. We tell ourselves and each other that we are responding to the difficult mind states that arise—greed, anger, fear, confusion—but sometimes we think that simply seeing the problem should be enough to break it up. We should regard seeing or awareness as being the first signal toward inner change, and not the final means to it.

RESTRAINING We may have to make our inner practice one of restraint. For example, if we experience a difficulty with a particular person, every time we see them, we might get upset and angry and end up saying things that later we regret. It not only makes our life difficult but we also make the life

of the other person difficult as well. This creates the need for the practice of restraint. The same principle also applies to greed, negativity, unhealthy habits, and so on.

We are sometimes afraid that if we show restraint, then we will suppress our problems and create even more difficulties. When we identify with this view, it becomes all too easy to give license to the mind to do what it wants. We might get the idea that if we follow through with an addiction, it will exhaust itself through wilful overuse—whether it is ice-cream, cigarettes, chocolate, spending money, or sex. We think: "I will go out and get what I want until I have had enough of it. I will then get sick of it."

We might believe that indulgence rather than restraint exhausts the desires. However, we may lose the taste for ice-cream for the rest of our life through indulgence, but it means that the force of unrestrained desire will only move onto something else. Indulgence does not resolve desire, nor is the object of desire the issue, but the desire itself is the problem. In an honest self-examination, we inquire into ourselves where we need to practice restraint. The recognition for this may come from us or it may come from feedback from others, but the practice of wise restraint can protect us from much suffering.

When we work on ourselves, we give support to others. We place less pressure on them, helping to make their lives easier. When we support the inner development of others, we give support to ourselves. Observing this, the Buddha said: "Who guards himself, guards others; who guards others, guards himself."

It is very important that we hear feedback from others so that we sit up and take notice of what they have to say about us. It will probably be a struggle for us to overcome our particular desire until the strength of the desire has run its course and has exhausted itself. This practice means that at appropriate times we are willing and able to apply restraint to what we want to see, hear, smell, taste, touch, or think about. We find a genuine inner contentment and satisfaction in overcoming unhealthy patterns of the mind through practicing restraint. When we do this we experience at first hand the principle that long-term benefits outlast short-term pleasure.

MAKING USE OF   This practice applies to things that we use. It includes the wide range of household goods, food, and medicine. If the mind experiences a state of dissatisfaction, we easily get tired of what we have and want to move onto something else. There is an unwillingness to make use of what is immediate, and there is also the tendency to pursue the latest fashion, gimmick, or technological development. We seem to lose our capacity to make use of what we have and want to go onto the latest advancement.

An obvious example of this arises for people who use computers. We buy the latest, fastest computer on the market. Six weeks later, our fast, new computer is outdated, as even faster computers become available. We forget to use what we have and get caught up with wanting the latest machine or software.

I remember in the 1970s one Buddhist center, the Insight Meditation Retreat center in Massachusetts, USA, put on a full program of retreats each year, with 50 to 100 people taking part. There were no computers, no databases, no network stations, no emails, no fax machines, and a small volunteer staff. Today there are directors and a management team and the center uses about a dozen sophisticated computers but it seems that more people complain about being overworked than twenty years ago. This situation is typical of organizations all over the world.

Another area of expenditure concerns energy. We need to make our cars last, but we also need to make use of public transport. We should take care with heating the home to conserve energy. We should hang washing up to dry indoors (such as in the bathroom) or outdoors, rather than waste energy on using a dryer that consumes a lot of energy. We can even turn the tap off while we brush our teeth and turn it back on only to rinse our mouth to make use of the water rather than waste it. Careful behavior to conserve energy resources at every level develops a different consciousness that contributes to overcoming personal, social, and global problems associated with abuse of resources. It is important to remember that the earth serves as our basic capital with resources of land, water, and air. We are now destroying it to the extent that UN officials say that future wars will not be over land but drinking water.

ENDURING   The most common form of endurance is of physical pain. Surgery, medication, and painkillers may eliminate the pain as well as giving unwanted side effects. In England, we sometimes use the proverb: "What cannot be cured must be endured."

Endurance of the pain requires a steadfast patience, the practice of taking one day at a time, an ability to accept what is without getting depressed. The capacity to endure, the development of resilience, protects us from getting overwhelmed, miserable, or suicidal. We have to acknowledge that the change from health to sickness, due to injury or an accident, can occur in a split second, through no fault of our own.

There are other forms of endurance as well. For example, we may have to patiently endure what we see—such as a large tree in a neighbour's garden that causes a shadow over our lawn. We may have to endure noise from a nearby building site or a smell from a local factory. It may be necessary to express our concerns, verbally or in the written form, but we still may have to endure the impact on our senses. If we cannot stay steady, then irritation, anger, or despair easily arises. At such times we have given what we see, hear, or smell authority over our inner life.

We may have to endure blame, fault-finding, and negativity from another that goes on and on. The other person finds it necessary to vilify us at every opportunity, but if we react in a similar way, we have sunk to that person's level. The Buddha encouraged us to practice equanimity to make our mind like the earth; it endures all manner of abuse from industrial pollution to throwing litter on the ground.

We can practice the art of a patient endurance in simple matters such as standing in line, experiencing delays in flights, tolerating changes in the minds of others, losing our income, and so on. We may have to endure wet weather on holiday and failing an exam after years of study. There is wisdom in learning to be with what is from day to day without getting downhearted because of the way events unfold.

If we indulge in alcohol or drugs, we make ourselves vulnerable to losing clarity and balance of mind.

AVOIDING   There is avoidance that is wise and there is avoidance that is unwise. A simple example of wise avoidance concerns the alcoholic in recovery who avoids the pub or parties where alcohol is freely available. It only takes one moment of impulsive action for weeks or even years of wise avoidance of alcohol to be lost. We may need to avoid the company of people who have addictive, possessive, or dominant personalities. Their way of life may conflict with our inner sensitivities, and due to our own patterns, we may find ourselves under the negative influence of others. We may need to avoid a particular individual if they have threatened us in a particular way.

When we were children, we may have avoided burning ourselves through having touched a hot coal or hot saucepan. We certainly learn quickly through such experiences about what can hurt us. Sometimes, we rely upon others to advise us about what to avoid to save ourselves hardship. There is a wealth of common-sense suggestions in society that can help us to live sensibly, happily, and expansively. We simply have to avoid what causes us harm and cultivate what helps us to handle situations skillfully.

At times, too, we have to rely upon ourselves if we are unable to find the necessary insights around us. Whatever the source, inner or outer, that advises us to avoid causing harm, we still have to follow it through. Those who follow it through show wisdom and those that ignore the signs show foolishness. At any time, with genuine awareness, we can transform a situation from foolishness to wisdom by making each act count.

REMOVING   Is there too much going on in our life? Do we feel overworked? Do we feel overwhelmed? Is there an accumulation of clutter around us? Are there unfinished tasks? Is there no opportunity for rest? If so, this imbalance means we need to remove some of these problems from our life. We forlornly imagine that we can carry on as before and find inner peace at the same time. The relationship between what we do and our inner life is inseparable.

Often small changes can make a difference to how we feel. For example, when we travel we have a tendency to carry far too much on a flight. We know that airlines often turn a blind eye to thirty kilos of luggage or more, even though the regulations only permit twenty kilos. We have the opportunity to make our life much easier, less frantic, so that we experience, as the Buddha said, a "calm abiding" in our daily lives.

The Buddha also emphasized removing that which "poisons" our inner life when we are caught up in selfishness, negativity, and worry, which can lead to blinding egotism, rage, or terror. Sometimes we poison our inner life and situations around us drop by drop over a period of time.

The Buddha compares this situation to a thatched roof. As the rain falls on such a roof, it becomes more and more sodden. If it is neglected over a period of time, the roof absorbs more and more water until it becomes damp, moldy, and unable to do its job of resisting the rain at all.

We practice to keep the mind firm, steady, and resolute from one day to the next so that we do not get weighed down with issues. Otherwise we will collapse through the weight of our neglect of our inner life. Removing is a practice of eliminating unnecessary thinking, opinions, and views, dispelling

PRACTICES FOR TODAY 2

1

Make a commitment today not to cause any harm

2

Be protective of all creatures, on the ground, in the water, or in the air

3

Adopt the view today of "live and let live" as a practice of nonharming

4

Walk gently on the earth today

5

Experience today free from conflict with any living being

Mindfulness of walking is a deeply valuable spiritual practice. Removing shoes gives us contact with the earth.

resentment through looking at a situation afresh, and removing worry about the future through practicing living one day at a time.

DEVELOPING   The six previous considerations can seem like a challenge to work with until we have overcome some of the difficulties that arise, but the quiet continuity of practice will make inroads into the inner life. The Buddha reminds us that we need to remember life outside problems so that we can respond happily to such awareness. That does not deny problems but simply puts them firmly in their place.

What do we enjoy? What do we appreciate? What makes things worthwhile? Even if the future seems uncertain and the past rather dark and difficult, we can find glimmers of light and joy and develop those. We can walk along the road bogged down in our internal world or open up our eyes to the colors of the new day. To let in enjoyable sounds and colors may not provide the delight that we would normally know when life flows along well, but what matters is the willingness to be open to the everyday things until we feel inner change coming about.

Practice means developing the heart and mind until we know and experience a genuine sense of moving on from a situation in terms of our attitude and outlook. In such a development, a burden, like a sack of potatoes, gradually becomes lighter. There is renewed energy and confidence to deal with what life brings us. Friendship, service to others, appreciation, love, generosity, kindness, compassion, and equanimity are all found in the heart.

If we give these qualities an important place in our life, we will experience a resolve to meet problems directly or to look outside of them to the wider world, knowing that the capacity to do this affects the very problems themselves. In such an approach, good humor about our life and circumstances can return, even if we know inside that the struggle will continue for years ahead.

We all know that happiness is mysterious, but we can say with inner confidence that it springs from a depth of inner peace. So let us keep our eyes, ears, and heart open to the wondrous incidental details of existence. The ordinary matters and so does our exposure to it. We can then cultivate a joyful connection with daily life and overcome difficulties. Then all our effort is truly worthwhile.

We treasure some of our family snaps. It is not always easy to communicate well with family members.

Meditation on Liberation

Use the upright sitting posture to read slowly through the following meditation. Liberation and inner joy show the consummation of living wisely. There is a path for living wisely and there are the profound fruits of the path.

Liberation stands beyond all circumstances
Nobody can give it, nobody can take it away
Liberation does not reside in any particular place
Nor is it found through any particular method, religion
* or philosophy*
It does not depend on such things for its abiding
* presence in our lives*
Let me meditate on this deeply
Let insights flow out of my being so that I can know
* what sages of past and present know who have*
* dissolved the sufferings and sorrows associated with*
* this world*
And abide easily with a freedom of spirit that knows
* no limits regardless of events that unfold in this world*
Let me aspire to realize this priceless and immeasurable
* freedom so that my self does not become the measure*
* of all things nor my thoughts and words become*
* thickening views*
In this vast freedom, I will know through my experience
* my life fits in easily with something much greater*

Meditation on Love Toward Three Kinds of People

Remember to practice these meditations regularly for all three kinds of people. At times, you will need to concentrate on just one of them. When you say the lines to each kind of person, remember to bring in the feeling of the heart to go with the words. It can be worthwhile memorizing the lines, or similar lines, to enable a loving presence to be steady in the heart whenever we are in contact with any of the three kinds of people.

To Your Loved Ones

May I always acknowledge and understand your
* intentions*
May I always be supportive for you in times of need
May I never place demands and pressure on you
May you be well and happy
May your life know contentment and joy
May you be peaceful and steady from one day to
* the next*
May our love and friendship for each other
* remain steady*

To Strangers

May I not rush to judgment on meeting you
May I show friendship and presence for you
May I communicate clearly and wisely in your presence
May your day be rich and worthwhile
May you act mindfully and consciously in all things
May everybody treat you with respect
May you show kindness to everybody that you meet
May your day be free from fear and worry
May you sleep well and peacefully tonight

To the Unfriendly

May your anger and resentment subside quickly
May you understand the pain you cause yourself
* and others*
May you find fresh ways to explore differences
May you see into the fear behind the anger
May you develop equanimity when things do not go
* your way*
May others stop being angry toward you
May you realize that anger does not cease with anger
May others listen to you and may you listen to others

141

Mindfulness of Spiritual Experiences

A person's ethics are known through
spending a long time with that person
and through not being inattentive.
A person's fortitude is known
through the way that person handles adversity.
A person's wisdom is known over a long time
through discussing with that person matters of importance.

THE BUDDHA

We have the capacity to discover and experience deep spiritual feelings about life on earth. It would be a pity to pass through life without an exposure to such experiences and realizations. The path of the Buddha is a spiritual path as much as it is practical and pragmatic. The Buddha compared the path to cutting one's way through the jungle (of discontent) until one reaches a clearing. He also compared the path to a boat to take one from the shore of problematic life to the shore of wisdom, freedom, and joy.

The purpose of this chapter is to remind you of the importance of finding exposure to spiritual experiences, through nature, meditation, and contact with others so that these kinds of experiences become a feature of your life, rather than nonexistent or a once-in-a-lifetime event.

Genuine spiritual experiences not only open up consciousness and challenge egotism in any form, but also point the way to a liberated life. We have much to discover. Through the range of experiences and insights, we will begin to understand and integrate into our experience a true and steadfast reality that formerly seemed distant and far-removed from our experience. We can know the Buddha mind in the middle of daily life.

The two meditations in this chapter are *Meditation on the Buddha* and *Meditation on Daily Life*.

There is much to appreciate about trees. They provide us with houses, furniture, firewood, shade, and are home to birds and insects. Our love and appreciation for trees tends to come alive when we feel connected to them. Trees can be metaphors for the spiritual life, and with mindfulness of spiritual awareness, if you want to get to the root of things you have to be like a tree. You have to be still and allow yourself to go deep, but it is all too easy to spend your life caught up in the leaves, branches, twigs, and even the fruit of the tree. You may wish to climb to the highest point in your particular field but that is no compensation for getting to the root of matters. You can be aware of going out on a limb, but there is a danger that the branch can break. If we are grounded and know our roots, we will not be easily blown over by circumstances.

WISE ATTENTION

All the time you reach out you lack the ability to stop still and reach within. You need to touch the source of your existence. If you track back deep enough, you will discover the depth of your being, free from the problems life brings. If you go on ignoring this, you will live trapped in the ego's determination to carry out what it wants. You are turning your back on what is real and what actually matters.

If you keep focusing on goals, you will lead a distracted life. An authentic step in daily life is going backward as well as forward. You keep on going forward in the vain hope it will lead somewhere. You may accumulate more possessions, labor-saving goods and devices, but remain stuck. Such goals do not lead anywhere, and upgrading your lifestyle certainly will not inform you about what it means to be alive on this earth, nor get you back to the source.

To make changes is a serious undertaking. It is not just a matter of trying to live a little bit more sanely amid a collective madness. It means cutting out as many of the superficial distractions as possible to make way for a whole new set of priorities.

THE SPIRIT FOR CHANGE

In the past twenty years, I have had the opportunity to listen to countless stories of people's lives. This leaves me with a tremendous sense of wonder and appreciation for people who have the courage to make changes despite opposition. Some people have stepped out of secure situations in order to experience an insecure way of living in this world. Others have taken steps to follow their dreams, although it seemed absurd to the rest of the world. Others have not only come to terms with a life-threatening illness but have turned their whole attention around, and come to see the illness as a blessing rather than a curse.

It is hard to imagine what moves the spirit of such people in this way. It is sometimes equally difficult for the people concerned to work out the reasons why they took the leap from the known into the unknown. What leaps have you made? You think your mind is full, that it is overflowing with feelings, thoughts, and numerous mental states, and the expression of your inner life seems to confirm how full your mind is. In fact this is not the only way of looking at your own mind.

If you keep focusing on the content of your mind, you will not appreciate how empty it really is—it is this which allows the diversity of content. Every expression of what is going on in your mind confirms that at the root it is empty. The emptiness of the mind confirms repeatedly the fullness of the mind.

If you spend more time contemplating the emptiness of the mind, you will appreciate it increasingly. You will come to feel less and less concerned with your changing states of mind, and this will allow the mind to return naturally to its original condition. The natural emptiness of the mind offers you the freedom to change many things about yourself.

Saints and sages of all traditions have encouraged us to spend time in nature, free from everyday cares.

Spiritual awareness and the arts have much to offer each other as contact with life's creative process.

CREATIVITY

A man said to the Buddha that if he was to develop spiritual awareness he first had to have the answers to certain questions. He asked, "I want to know how did this world begin? I want to know how this world is going to end? I must know whether or not I will exist after death."

The Buddha asked, "Did I say I would give you these answers? Did I ever promise to tell you the answers to these questions? These questions are not really the concern of the spiritual life, and they are not conducive to awareness, depth, nonattachment, and the discovery of liberation."

Creativity, nature, and spirituality have a common relationship: each one represents a contact and intimacy with the unfolding process of life. You can ask yourself: in what ways do I express creativity in my daily life? How much real exposure do I have to nature? In what ways do I make contact with a variety of spiritual experiences?

Creativity flows out of the depth of our being and expresses itself in life. It is wholesome and healthy to find ways to bring the creative into unfolding existence. We may experience some bursts of creative energy but then it quickly fades away until we experience another inspiration. The gaps between these bursts of creativity can be far too long. One percent inspiration, ninety-nine percent perspiration carries a certain truth!

Sometimes, the experience of creativity comes joyfully, effortlessly, and there is an extraordinary high flow of energy. We do not feel that we have anything to do with this creative force, it seems like the creative outflow is just running through us. We experience ourselves as a vehicle for such creativity rather than the agent. Of course it is all too easy for the ego to grasp on to the creative flow and boost itself up through thinking of itself as the vehicle. Nevertheless, if we look deeper, we realize there is nothing for the ego to grasp onto, that there is only the flow of creativity itself.

At other times the act of creativity seems extraordinarily difficult. There is a feeling of resistance, lack of initiative, and a tremendous amount of hard work and effort to bring forth a creative expression. It seems sometimes that neither the heart, mind, nor body want to cooperate together to be creative. In this case, discipline is important. Discipline and training in

meditation work well together, and we may need a meditation group or to participate in intensive retreats, to experience sustained discipline.

The meditation practice of bringing the attention back to the breathing, back to the here and now, and cutting off distractions is an expression of inner discipline. This serves as a real training for the mind. With this training, we can then apply a focused attention to our chosen expression of creativity.

NATURE

The Buddha loved the outdoors. He loved walking through the various small nations scattered in northern India, and encouraged respect for the environment and all living creatures. Today, we see the impact of human behavior on land, water, and air. The force of human desire affects personal, social, and

The Buddha encouraged people to spend as much time as possible outdoors in nature.

147

global life at an ever-increasing cost to nature. The size of cities and consequent pollution is constantly increasing while villages shrink in numbers as young people go to the cities to look for work, and there is the loss of community.

It takes a certain determination to put ourselves back in touch with nature so we enjoy the experience of the sky above our heads and the earth beneath our feet. I often think of the sky as my father and the earth as my mother. We need to feel close to our natural environment, to the hills and valleys, trees and flowers, and in a very real way return to our roots. Environmentalists tell us that tens of thousands of years ago we emerged out of the rainforests and began to settle on open land to start the first farms. It seems that as the centuries have gone by we have become more and more alienated from the natural world.

This alienation from the natural environment contributes significantly to the exploitation of our natural resources. To bring a spiritual awareness to nature means to respect our environment, to develop deep intimacy through contact, and wise use of resources in our personal lives.

It takes commitment and quiet discipline to spend a lot of time outdoors in parks and open environments so that we genuinely develop a love and appreciation for the natural world. We do not have to explain to ourselves or to others our love of the outdoor life, nor do we have to limit ourselves to being outdoors when the weather is clement.

In spending time outdoors, there are three senses that are in moment-to-moment use: seeing, listening, and feeling. When we are outdoors we need to remember to observe the general sweep of what comes to our eyes as well as the particular—a flower, tree, bird, or insect. We bring our awareness to nature in order to feel our participation in it. At times we enjoy a long, unbroken view, whether in the open countryside, in the mountains, or by the sea. These perspectives remind us that we are not lords of the earth, nor is nature our servant, nor do we have some inalienable right to do what we like with it. Life is "enviro-mental," and we must use our minds to appreciate it. We are one of countless expressions of nature and all of it is coparticipating together.

In the Buddhist tradition there is constant reference to the importance of contact with the elements. The Buddha sat under a tree, meditated, and suddenly realized what really matters in terms of human beings' relationships to existence. Generations of men and women in the Buddhist tradition have actively pursued the outdoor way of life to feel close to themselves and close to the world that surrounds them. For many centuries Buddhist monks and nuns have traveled the length and breadth of their native lands by foot to keep alive the natural intimacy of contact with nature. Such an approach to life contributes significantly to a healthy body, healthy mind, and deep inner sense of well-being.

We may not have the opportunity, or the privilege, of such a free-spirited way of life, but we certainly can take steps to redress the imbalance that keeps us within closed walls, living in the shadow of concrete and high-rise buildings and glued to the television or computer screen morning, noon, and night. It ought to be obvious to us that while we enjoy the benefits of materialism, we have gone to an extreme in that direction. We have become hopelessly out of touch with the wonder and the miracle of the natural world. Living wisely does not neglect this way of living; close contact with nature and ourselves on a regular basis go together like wood and trees.

SPIRITUALITY

The Buddha reminded us that our inner life makes its impact directly on the world around us. If we change inwardly, the outer world will change as well. Occasionally we might make some comment to others or ourselves about the importance of touching something spiritual in our life, but spirituality is extremely hard to define and seems rather remote from the bare actualities of getting on with our life. So it can be useful to stop and check in with ourselves from time to time about our degree of interest, if any, in spirituality. Wisely, the Buddhist tradition has encouraged as well as detailed the value and range of deep spiritual experiences.

Some of us have a knee-jerk reaction that dismisses anything spiritual as irrelevant to daily life and out of touch with the real world. Such a view may show that we remain bereft of any spiritual experiences. If we feel we have never had any kind of spiritual experience, we might need to place ourselves in an environment or a group that makes spiritual experience a priority. Most religious and spiritual traditions, ancient and contemporary, offer retreats. In the course of these retreats, the spiritual experience is total participation in the program or can be experienced as particular moments that may arise during the retreat.

Solitude also brings benefits. We may wonder why it is important to engage ourselves in that which we refer to as spiritual. The answer to this is not for somebody else to explain this to us but comes as a result of our own experience.

As much as possible, we need to act to protect the natural world from exploitation.

SIX PERFECTIONS

We can bring a deep spiritual sensitivity to our activities at home. Some people cultivate this by setting aside a sacred space at home to include religious symbols, beautiful flowers, incense, and perhaps an appropriate wall hanging. The main task of spiritual awareness is to bring deep inner qualities of life into day-to-day circumstances. However, the Buddhist tradition has referred to the importance of the six perfections:

❖ Generosity
❖ Morality
❖ Patience
❖ Energy
❖ Meditative concentration
❖ Wisdom

When we speak of these noble qualities of the inner life, we place them under the umbrella of spiritual awareness. This means that we value every one of them and make a commitment to cultivate and develop each of them, to overcome and avoid those states of mind that obstruct the expression of any of the six perfections.

These six perfections relate to the circumstances of our daily life. Through developing them, we can experience fulfillment, though obviously there is always room for further development of any of the perfections. There is a genuine sense that we practice to bring each one to fulfillment in a nonegotistical way. This is why it is called a perfection.

It means, for example, that when we have fully developed the quality of patience it has become a natural response to a situation where in the past we would have become impatient. Patience means that we can remain firm and steady through a slow-moving situation, even if the circumstance carries on much longer than we would wish. We practice to abide in the here and now, even when we are in the most trying of circumstances.

The six perfections remind us to work diligently on our inner life so that we truly evolve as a human being. It is part of our sense of inner responsibility to work on ourselves. One of the significant benefits of practicing all of the six perfections is how it brings a depth of inner peace to our lives and the willingness to challenge ourselves rather than go along with some of our old unsatisfactory patterns. Through the range of meditation practices and teachings involving the six perfections we experience a genuine enhancement of our inner life and a natural sense of freedom.

All of this inner work does not operate in a vacuum, and we do not work on ourselves just for the sake of it or to get along with life a little easier. There is a much greater challenge; there is another way of looking at our inner state that has another dimension to it altogether.

PRACTICES FOR TODAY 1

1

Take the initiative today to touch upon the spiritual

2

Research any workshops or retreats you may like to attend

3

Find a beautiful passage in a spiritual text and read it out loud

4

Spend some time looking at the night sky from your window or outdoors

5

Reflect on the wonder and mystery of existence

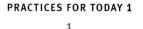

A natural setting, such as a garden or a park, can provide a wonderful setting for calm and relaxed reflection on the wonder of life.

Buddhist monks living in the Himalayas hang prayer flags such as these in their monasteries.

As human beings, we feel proud of some of the extraordinary technological developments that the human mind has accomplished during the course of its evolution. We only have to look at the world around us. For example, I was speaking to a friend, Ram, who is a poor *chai wallah* (he runs a tea stall) in Bodh Gaya, India. I had in my hand a handwritten letter. I explained to him that I was going to a nearby shop to fax the letter to my daughter in England.

I explained to him that I placed the piece of paper in the fax machine, pressed the numbers on the fax to link up with the telephone, and simultaneously everything on that piece of paper appeared on a piece of paper on the other side of the world. At first, he thought I was pulling his leg. He could not comprehend how the words written on a sheet of paper could reproduce in exactly the same way on a piece of paper thousands of miles away. I equally find it extraordinary; it is totally beyond my comprehension, just like the *chai wallah*.

151

SPIRITUAL EVOLUTION

We have evolved in terms of the numerous skills and wealth of knowledge we now have at our disposal. Sometimes they are put to good use for the welfare of others, but sadly they are also put to destructive use. Spiritual evolution concerns consciousness. It is one thing to use the mind to create sophisticated forms of technology for our habitat, work environment, and modes of transport, but it is equally important for consciousness to evolve in our minds in order for us to experience transcendental insights and touch upon the deepest truths.

Evolution of spiritual consciousness means that our heart expands into unstoppable expressions of love, deep friendship, compassion, and joy. As yet, our society has concentrated so much on physical and biological evolution that we have not realized the profound importance of the evolution of consciousness. An evolved consciousness leaves behind

A full consciousness brings spiritual joy, happiness, and compassion.

PRACTICES FOR TODAY 2

1

Reflect on the emptiness of egotism

2

In what moments do you feel free?

3

What contributes to your sense of expansiveness, of having no limitations?

4

What do you need to do to enlighten your life?

5

Would it be useful to develop further some of the teachings and practices found in this book?

Look into a sunny sky and watch the clouds—freedom is defined by moments like this.

the forces of greed, hate, and delusion. If we develop and evolve through spiritual awareness, the inner life will transform as much as the technology of global communication that has developed over the last two generations. The time has come to generate an authentic spiritual renaissance so that we emerge out of the dark shadows of a rigid, hedonistic, and enslaved society dedicated to the pursuit of ownership above all else. Instead we explore what it means to wake up truly. Let us show a profound and deep connection with all things so that we act wisely in a variety of ways.

The Buddha was once lying under the tree at Kushinagar in India. It was the final night of the full moon in May some 2,500 years ago and the Buddha was dying. A man named Supabadha came to the Buddha but before he could reach him, Ananda, the Buddha's attendant, stopped him. "Do not disturb him," he said to Supabadha. "His body is breathing its last." Supabadha said, "But I have a question, I must ask this question."

The Buddha heard this conversation taking place and he said to Ananda, "Let this man come. If I can, I will answer the question." The man said, "There are so many voices of authority. Some claim they are enlightened. How can I know?"

The Buddha replied, "Don't concern yourself with this question. See into yourself; see the Dharma for yourself. Work out your liberation."

THE IMMEASURABLE

Our mind has a certain capacity to comprehend specific situations, whether we like them or not. Yet, we have access to profound experiences that go beyond the mind's comprehension. We may find the sweet touch of the Immeasurable through a variety of ways, including meditation, and simply being with nature. We may experience a sudden moment that takes us out of our ordinary mind and puts us firmly in touch with this enduring mystery—the mystery that remains totally incomprehensible to the everyday mind. These experiences have the potential to have a profoundly beneficial influence on our daily life. They can put many things into perspective.

You will benefit from a precious feeling of traveling wisely through this world. You will not lose yourself in possessions, roles, and future plans; you will make yourself available to experience dimensions of the breathtaking mystery that knows no limitations. Consequently, everything else falls into place in the scheme of things. You will experience daily freedom and a truly liberated way of life.

You can take inspiration from knowing that others have taken risks to realize an enlightened life, including Prince Siddhartha Gautama, the Buddha. Is it your turn?

The night sky brings clarity of thought and mind to enlightened people.

Meditation on the Buddha

Read the following meditation slowly and mindfully to allow yourself to absorb whatever seems appropriate. The purpose of this meditation is to break free from the mindset that makes us think that things are only as we see them. The world appears flat but that does not make it flat. A person appears to be in an up-and-down mood but that does not make them up and down. If we look deeply enough, we will know that the true nature of a person abides without measure, without limitations. To see this is to see the Buddha. After this meditation on the Buddha, be still and quiet for several minutes.

The Buddha died at the foot of a tree in May. It is said that petals fell to form a carpet around him.

*Just as the sun shines, despite the clouds so all
    beings are enlightened, despite the issues
Let me acknowledge this
All beings are liberated
Let me acknowledge this
All beings are grounded in the Truth
Let me witness this
Everybody is a Buddha
Let me be respectful to everybody
Let me not be deceived by the superficial conditioning
    of others
So that I have no doubt that greed, hate, and delusion
    remain empty of substance
So that I have no doubt that boredom, anxiety, and
    fear stand empty of reality
Let myself not be deceived with such impressions
May I end preoccupation with the mind states of others
May I see the abiding Buddha nature in everybody even
    in times of difficulty and disagreement
May I realize that all beings share the same
    undivided nature
May my communications and actions reveal
    this understanding
Just as the Buddha is revealed equally everywhere
May I be mindful of the world as a Buddha abides
    mindfully of the world*

A Daily Meditation

Look around your home and find what you feel is the best spot for regular meditation. Place the items that you feel would enhance that place, for example a mat, a sacred object, a flower, a candle, a small bell, or just a chair, or meditation cushion. To begin the meditation, play some meditative music. Read out loud from a book that you appreciate, or play an extract from a taped talk on meditation or spiritual teachings. Bring your mindfulness to your breathing. Practice initially for 15 minutes and extend your daily meditation times up to 45 minutes. You can practice once a day, or twice a day, morning and evening.

I am breathing in
I am breathing out
I am breathing in a long breath
I am breathing out a long breath
I am aware of the breath as it comes into my body
I am aware of the breath as it leaves my body
I am aware of the in-breath as it enters my nose
I am aware of the in-breath as it goes into my lungs
I am aware of the finish of the in-breath
I am aware of the out-breath as it departs from my nose
I am aware of the out-breath as it departs from my lungs
I am aware of the process of life
I am at ease with the process of life
I am free amid the process of life

A full lotus position is wonderful, but difficult to achieve. Sit how you are comfortable when meditating.

About the Author

Christopher Titmuss has been teaching insight meditation and spiritual awakening around the world for the past 25 years. He is a cofounder of Gaia House, an international Buddhist retreat center in Devon, England.

Christopher spent about ten years in the East between 1967 and 1977, including six years as a Buddhist monk in Thailand and India. He is a founder member of the 12-strong international board of the Buddhist Peace Fellowship. In 1986 and 1992, he stood for Parliament for the Green Party.

Christopher is the author of ten books on spiritual practice, including *Light on Enlightenment, The Power of Meditation,* and *The Buddha's Book of Daily Meditations.*

For program and newsletter of retreats, workshops, and teachings worldwide contact:

Gaia House
West Ogwell
near Newton Abbot
Devon TQ12 6EN
England

Tel 44 (0) 1626 333613
Fax 44 (0) 1626 352680

Email gaiahouse@gn.apc.org
Website www.insightmeditation.org

FURTHER READING *Books by Christopher Titmuss*

SPIRIT FOR CHANGE (£5.99, $10). *166 pages. Published by Green Print, available from Insight Books, c/o Gaia House*

Many people who engage in the struggle for social change also have powerful spiritual commitments. The author talks to 14 people about their motivations that inspired them to take action. They offer constructive responses to difficult and painful situations.

FREEDOM OF THE SPIRIT (£6.99, $11). *180 pages. Published by Green Print, London, available from Insight Books, c/o Gaia House*

The author meets with another 15 men and women from different backgrounds to discuss their commitments and their roots in their religious faith.

FIRE DANCE AND OTHER POEMS (£4.99, $8.00). *112 pages. Published by Insight Books (Totnes), distributed by Wisdom Books, London*

This is a collection of 86 poems exploring such themes as love, meditation, change, death, and liberation.

THE PROFOUND AND THE PROFANE (£7.95, $14.95). *192 pages. Published by Insight Books (Totnes), distributed by Wisdom Books, London*

The author directs his inquiry into the depths of the spiritual life. This book is intended for those who wish to understand the place of spirituality in daily life and whose highest priority is enlightenment. Themes include the nature of awareness, insight, relationship to perception, and awakening to the immeasurable.

THE GREEN BUDDHA (£11, $18). *302 pages. Published by Insight Books (Totnes), distributed by Wisdom Books, London*

In a bold and uncompromising exploration, the author challenges the forces and influences of the ego—in the personal, corporate, environmental, and political life. He draws upon his experiences for profound change, the teachings of the Buddha and the relevance of spirituality to national and global issues.

LIGHT ON ENLIGHTENMENT (£9.99, $15.95). *220 pages. Rider Books, Random House, London, and Shambhala Books, USA, November, 1999*

The themes examined in this book address every feature of our daily lives. There are many stories and anecdotes throughout the book. The book takes the form of a modern-day commentary on such essential teachings as the Four Noble Truths, the Triple Gem, the Four Foundations of Awareness, the Four Divine Abidings and the Four Noble Ones. The book also includes specific practices for daily life and areas for inquiry.

THE POWER OF MEDITATION (£10.99, $16.95). *112 pages. Published by Apple Press, London, and Sterling Publishing Co, New York, October, 1999*

This large-format book contains comprehensive meditation instructions and practices suitable for numerous daily life situations. There are more than 100 photographs and illustrations. They include photographs of the author in the primary postures—sitting, walking, standing, and reclining—and scenes from nature. There are detailed meditation instructions on mindfulness of breathing, body awareness, lovingkindness, and observation of thought. The book comes with a free CD of music for various meditations.

THE LITTLE BOX OF INNER CALM (£10.99, $16.95). *Packaged by Quarto Press, London. Published by Barrons Educational Publishers, New York*

This package contains practical instructions and guidance for clarity and inner peace in daily life. Along with beautiful illustrations and photographs, *The Little Box* also contains a mala, incense, a prayer, printed mandala, and small bell of mindfulness.

AN AWAKENED LIFE (£9.99, $15.95). *Published by Rider Books, Random House, London, and Shambhala Books, USA*

Drawing on the deep discoveries of the Buddhist tradition, Christopher says we spend far too much time in superficial preoccupations and not enough time looking deeply into things. He points to an uninhibited life amidst the pressures of everyday activity.

THE BUDDHA'S BOOK OF DAILY MEDITATIONS (£8.99). *Published by Rider Books, Random House, London*

A daily quote from the Buddha's teachings for 365 days. The selections embrace the practical and the inspirational. This diary includes numerous well-known statements by the Buddha on all aspects of living as well as poetic expressions of his love of the deep things of daily life.

All above books are available from

Insight Books (Totnes)
c/o Gaia House
West Ogwell
near Newton Abbot
Devon TQ12 6EN
England
Tel 44 (0) 1626 333613

(please add £2.50 for post and package for overseas mailing)

Index

ACKNOWLEDGMENTS

I wish to express my deepest appreciation to the Buddha and to the down-to-earth wisdom found in the Theravada Buddhist tradition of Thailand. My gratitude particularly goes to Venerable Ajahn Dhammadaro and the late Venerable Ajahn Buddhadasa for their teachings during my six years as a Buddhist monk in Thailand.

I wish to thank the Green Party for its commitment to the welfare of people and our environment.

I also wish to express gratitude to Nina Wedborn of Stockholm, Sweden, for her support and insights in helping me prepare the outline for each chapter of *Buddhist Wisdom for Daily Living*. Nina's countless suggestions made the task of writing the book much easier. Thanks also to Anne Ashton, my secretary, for her ongoing assistance throughout the year. Gill Farrer-Halls kindly and sensitively edited *Buddhist Wisdom for Daily Living*. Also appreciation to my daughter, Nshorna; Judith, my sister; my mother, and friends in the spiritual life. Thanks also to the Buddhist Publication Society, (PO Box 61), Kandy, Sri Lanka, for permission to use quotes of the words of the Buddha from *The Life of the Buddha*, translated by Venerable Bhikkhu Nanamoli. The Buddhist Publication Society has worked tirelessly to make these important teachings of the Buddha available worldwide. Finally, I wish to express appreciation to Debbie Thorpe and Olivia Strand at Godsfield Press, and Sarah Bragginton at The Bridgewater Book Company, for their suggestions, editing, and book design.